EARLY LITERACY PROGRAMMING EN ESPAÑOL

Mother Goose on the Loose®

Programs for Bilingual Learners

Betsy Diamant-Cohen

Neal-Schuman Publishers, Inc.

New York   London

Published by Neal-Schuman Publishers, Inc.
100 William St., Suite 2004
New York, NY 10038

Library of Congress Cataloging-in-Publication Data

Diamant-Cohen, Betsy.
   Early literacy programming en español : Mother Goose on the Loose programs for bilingual learners / Betsy Diamant-Cohen.
      p. cm.
   Includes bibliographical references and indexes.
   ISBN 978-1-55570-691-3 (alk. paper)
   1. Children's libraries—Activity programs—United States. 2. Children's libraries—Services to Hispanic Americans. 3. Libraries and infants—United States. 4. Libraries and toddlers—United States. 5. Early childhood education—Activity programs—United States. 6. Nursery rhymes—Study and teaching (Early childhood)—Spanish speakers. 7. Education, Bilingual—United States. I. Title.

Z718.3.D53 2010
027.6'3—dc22

2009049594

Dedicated to Michael Cass-Beggs (1941–2007),

who generously encouraged the use of his mother's material

in all Mother Goose on the Loose® programs.

His unflagging enthusiasm and joy at seeing his mother's legacy renewed

inspired the writing of this Mother Goose on the Loose en Español™ manual.

Table of Contents

List of Illustrations

FIGURES

FLANNEL BOARD TEMPLATES

Foreword

Some years ago, the Massachusetts Board of Library Commissioners became aware of an exciting new program aimed at babies and caregivers called Mother Goose on the Loose (MGOL). It was quickly adopted as a successful model whereby we made federal grants available to our public libraries to carry out the program. For the past five years we have invited Betsy Diamant-Cohen each fall to provide hands-on training workshops that have afforded our librarians the knowledge, tools, and inspiration to start their own MGOL programs.

In the past few years, an increasing number of Spanish-speaking families have begun to participate in these programs, and some librarians have struggled with how best to reach out to this group of English-language learners. When I learned that a Spanish-language training of MGOL was being developed, I immediately asked Betsy if we could schedule a workshop in our state. Last fall, she presented the workshop to an enthusiastic audience, and, most heartening, as a result two libraries decided to utilize the adapted MGOL model with Latino families in their communities in the coming year.

The Mother Goose on the Loose en Español program was developed as a response to the need to provide modeling activities at the library that can be practiced at home in either Spanish or English. Utilizing the sound outreach technique of working with a community partner who is fluent or comfortable speaking Spanish, Betsy Diamant-Cohen has adapted her award-winning program to reach a new audience of children and families. Thus, any library that wishes to extend services to members of its Spanish-speaking community can embrace this program even if the librarian offering the program may lack those language skills.

Balancing translations in Spanish of the many wonderful original songs of the late Barbara Cass-Beggs, whose Listen, Like, Learn program so inspired Betsy, this new book, *Early Literacy Programming en Español: Mother Goose on the Loose® Programs for Bilingual Learners*, includes many traditional rhymes well-known throughout the Spanish-speaking community. Mother Goose on the Loose en Español incorporates both into a structured program that is developmentally sound and culturally relevant. The program also serves to respond to an emerging trend among parents whose first language is English who seek opportunities to introduce their young children to a bilingual experience. Designed to work in both Spanish and English, MGOL provides an opportunity for very young children to hear language at the time they are developing phonemic awareness. Based on proven techniques of using traditional songs and rhymes, simple picture books, and stories in English and bilingual formats, Mother Goose on the Loose en Español will contribute to vocabulary development in both languages. I strongly believe in the value of this program and am thrilled that this new model will allow librarians and early childhood providers to reach an even wider audience.

Shelley Quezada
Consultant, Library Services to the Unserved
Massachusetts Board of Library Commissioners
Boston, MA

Preface

Childhood studies continue to emphasize the idea that engaging young children with diverse forms of stimulation in a nurturing environment significantly facilitates development and educational success. *Early Literacy Programming en Español: Mother Goose on the Loose® Programs for Bilingual Learners* is a resource that follows this idea by helping librarians, whether Spanish speaking or not, create a high-quality Spanish-language Mother Goose on the Loose program within their library. This book provides the tools librarians and community partners need to create Spanish-language Mother Goose on the Loose programs that encourage healthy child development while providing an informal, inventive opportunity for parent–child education. Inside you will find the following resources:

- A companion multimedia CD-ROM that includes songs in both Spanish and English, along with customizable forms for program preparation
- A ready-to-present script in both Spanish and English
- Tips for working with Latino communities
- A summary of research on early literacy and bilingual language development
- Instructions for creating a unique series of programs
- Tools for assessment, evaluation, and program promotion
- Lyrics to songs and rhymes that work well in a Spanish-language Mother Goose on the Loose program
- And more!

Scope

The United States has always been a nation of immigrants. However, the recent surge in Latin American immigrants to both urban centers and nontraditional geographic regions is demanding social services be not only more inclusive but also more culturally and linguistically sensitive. The extent of this population surge makes headlines from time to time, and it is no surprise that the number of Spanish speakers in the United States is increasing. Libraries around the country have recognized the importance of reaching out to the Spanish-speaking population, and many have realized that children's Spanish-language programming is an effective way to not only bring the entire family into the library but also provide much-needed assistance to the Latino community in the areas of school preparation and English-language acquisition. *Early Literacy Programming en Español: Mother Goose on the Loose® Programs for Bilingual Learners*, which presents the successful program Mother Goose on the Loose en Español—also referred to as Escucha y Disfruta (Listen and Enjoy)—does just that.

Brief History and Description of Mother Goose on the Loose en Español

Mother Goose on the Loose is a 30-minute nursery rhyme program for children from birth to age three that seamlessly combines books, music, movement, play, art, and language with the development of social and emotional skills of young children, while also providing informal education on child development through tips for parents. Throughout the past five years, countless librarians throughout the United States have attended Mother Goose on the Loose training workshops and have brought the program to their libraries. The program's popularity stems from the ease with which librarians can learn and present it, the solid research supporting it, and the enthusiasm of the adults and children who participate in it.

The typical activities in an MGOL program promote an enthusiastic attitude toward books, offering children many opportunities to practice taking turns, following directions, being patient, and showing appreciation to others. During the program, librarians model book-reading behavior, present playful ways to use books, and give positive reinforcement, so that adults and children not only bond with their local librarians but also experience a sense of community and create relationships with other program attendees. In addition, MGOL programs help children develop many school readiness skills by encouraging them to build their vocabulary, use their imagination, and expand their creativity. These are just a few of the benefits of Mother Goose on the Loose, but they serve to illustrate why the program is currently offered by so many libraries, as well as in child care centers and by other caregivers with groups of children.

The Mother Goose on the Loose program combines principles of library programming with Barbara Cass-Beggs' Listen, Like, Learn approach for teaching music to young children. Mother Goose on the Loose is different from all other baby programs precisely because of its connection with Barbara Cass-Beggs (see Figure P.1).

Barbara Cass-Beggs (1904–1990) was a Canadian music educator who developed the Listen, Like, Learn approach to teach music to children, using music principles established by Kodály and Orff. Children are introduced to a piece of music by first listening to it. After hearing it (perhaps a number of times), it becomes familiar to them. Once they like it, they are more attentive and receptive to that particular piece of music

Figure P.1: Cass-Beggs at a Your Baby Needs Music Class in Jerusalem, Israel

and are thus able to learn from it. Barbara also took a holistic approach to children that included exposure to the arts with great respect for a child's individuality. Barbara incorporated her findings on child development and brain research with her methods for teaching music. In addition, she wrote songs and adapted others in order to create a number of age-appropriate activities specifically for children.

Through her two courses, Your Baby Needs Music and Your Child Needs Music, Barbara taught music to many children and their parents, while encouraging bonding, laughter, imagination, and teamwork. Through easy musical games, Barbara found ways to let parents observe and appreciate the developing skills of their growing children. I studied with Barbara in the late 1980s and became a certified instructor for Your Baby Needs Music classes using Barbara's Listen, Like, Learn approach. During this time, I was also working as a part-time English language librarian at the Ruth Youth Wing Library of the Israel Museum in Jerusalem. Because this museum library focused on children's book illustration, the storytime program focused more on exposing children to the art in books rather than on language. After a year of presenting weekly preschool storytimes at the museum library and Your Baby Needs Music classes at a local maternity hospital, I created a program for young children that combined Barbara's methodology with traditional library programming techniques for sharing high-quality books with children. The result: a blend of music, language, illustration, books, positive reinforcement, parent–child bonding, laughter, ritual, repetition with variety, parental tips, and high-energy activities paired with restful lullabies. This new program was called Mother Goose on the Loose. I ran the Mother Goose on the Loose program on a weekly basis for years in the Ruth Youth Wing Library of the Israel Museum in Jerusalem (see Figure P.2). During this time, I was able to tweak the program, constantly improving it. In addition, scientific findings provided additional support for the value of the program in promoting early literacy and school readiness skills.

I brought the program to the Enoch Pratt Free Library in Baltimore, Maryland, in 1999 and have been delighted to see it spread nationwide since then. Buena Casa, Buena Brasa (A Warm Home, A Warm Hearth) was a Spanish-language version of Mother Goose on the Loose developed and presented at the Enoch Pratt Free Library in Baltimore by Anne Calderón from the Maryland Committee for Children and me (see Figure P.3).

During the time of this program, some amazing developments occurred. After Buena Casa, Buena Brasa ran for more than a year, English-speaking parents and children started attending. English-speaking parents wanted to expose their children to Spanish. One English-speaking mom asked Anne if a Spanish-speaking mom was

Figure P.2: One of the Earliest Mother Goose on the Loose Programs at the Israel Museum in Jerusalem

Figure P.3: Buena Casa, Buena Brasa Thanksgiving at the Enoch Pratt Free Library, November 2007

willing to read a Spanish story to her child before each program. In return, the English-speaking mom offered to read a story in English to the Spanish speaker's child. Through this one request, quite a few bilingual story-reading pairs sprung up. Even now, this cultural literary exchange takes place at the beginning of each program. In addition to the benefit of hearing a story in another language read by a native speaker, comfortable and long-lasting relationships are being forged. For example, in my program, babies are held by everyone and children's names are known by everyone—there is no invisible dividing line between English and Spanish speakers.

Immigrants from countries where Spanish was not a prominent language also began attending the Buena Casa, Buena Brasa program, because it offered a community feeling where attendees felt comfortable. One woman from the Middle East, who could speak neither English nor Spanish, came on a weekly basis with her daughter and was warmly accepted into the community. The Middle Eastern woman became pregnant with her second child, and shortly before giving birth the Spanish-speaking women of the group threw her a baby shower!

In the second year of the program, one week before Thanksgiving, some women approached Anne and said, "We would like to celebrate Thanksgiving in America, and we have never done it before. Because our library friends are our best friends, we would like to have a Thanksgiving celebration here. Can we?" Although it was only two weeks before Thanksgiving, with help from many people in the Enoch Pratt Free Library, the celebratory meal was scheduled. One day before Thanksgiving families brought spouses, grandparents, uncles, and aunts. Rice, beans, tortillas, chili, and other Spanish dishes sat alongside Asian and Middle Eastern foods and the traditional turkey and pumpkin pie. At the end of the meal, we sang a song about pumpkin pie and then posed for a group picture (see Figure P.3). Spanish speakers chatted comfortably with English speakers and took turns holding each other's children. The day seemed magical.

Early Literacy Programming en Español: Mother Goose on the Loose® Programs for Bilingual Learners is an adaptation of the original Mother Goose on the Loose program that incorporates successful experiences with Buena Casa, Buena Brasa. Because it uses the same Cass-Beggs Listen, Like, Learn approach, Mother Goose on the Loose en Español can also be called "Escucha y Disfruta con Mamá Gansa," which translates as "Listen and Enjoy with Mother Goose." Using the basic Mother Goose on the Loose format, Escucha y Disfruta includes Spanish-language translations of songs and rhymes by Barbara Cass-Beggs and traditional Spanish-language children's activities. It also includes components geared for the cultural background of Hispanic participants. Developmental tips focus on information relevant to behavior in the public library, the resources available to Spanish speakers, and tips about bilingual language development. The other major difference between Mother Goose on the Loose and Mother Goose on the Loose en Español is a new focus on community. In the libraries where Anne and I ran Buena Casa, Buena Brasa, the majority of native Spanish-speaking participants were immigrants. Many parents and care providers arrived at the library feeling culturally and linguistically isolated. Our weekly meetings of parents in similar situations and interests became a strong, positive force in community building.

A typical Mother Goose on the Loose program is often followed by a 30-minute play period, during which children play with educationally appropriate toys, while adults converse. In Buena Casa, Buena Brasa, while children were occupied with free play, parents were given a short survey for the purpose of gathering data. Surveys were then followed by general announcements and a short family play period. Toys were then collected, tours of the library were given to newcomers, and, if planned in advance, a particular library service was highlighted. At the end of the program, everyone was invited to partake in refreshments. This successful model can be replicated in Mother Goose on the Loose en Español.

I designed this manual to provide everything needed to create a successful Spanish-language early literacy program. Because each community is different, you may find some of the material superfluous. For instance, information about integrating Spanish speakers into the library may not be relevant for you. In some communities where the local library lacks any Spanish-speaking staff, non-English speakers simply do not use the library. In other communities, even with no Spanish-speaking staff, non-English-speaking patrons feel comfortable using the library and may perhaps account for the bulk of the library's visitors.

Organization

Part I, "Things You Need to Know Before Starting a Mother Goose on the Loose en Español Program," offers three chapters of essential background information. If you would rather just dive right in and begin planning your program, go directly to the second part of the book.

Chapter 1, "Learning, Early Literacy, Spanish-Language Considerations, and Mother Goose on the Loose en Español," discusses research that led to the creation of this program and that supports the benefits of early literacy skills, ideas on multiple intelligences, and the development of school readiness skills. Issues surrounding the use of both spoken and written Spanish in the United States are considered. Variations in Spanish-language use among people from different parts of the world, as well as within the same country, are illuminated. Anne Calderón explains the Spanish-language choices for the translations within this book and for the Mother Goose on the Loose en Español script.

Chapter 2, "Bilingual Language Development," written by Gilda Martinez, PhD, addresses concerns regarding language acquisition for children of Spanish-speaking, non-English-speaking parents.

Chapter 3, "Working with the Latino Community," written by Anne Calderón, draws upon Anne's experiences with the Buena Casa, Buena Brasa program and provides tips about supplies, behavior expectations, and other helpful comments. If you are a Spanish-speaking librarian who is not going to be using a community partner to help run your programs, you may choose to skip this chapter.

Part II, "Planning for Mother Goose on the Loose en Español," features seven chapters that give all the tools necessary for running a Mother Goose on the Loose en Español program at your library. An explanation of the traits that make Mother Goose on the Loose different from all other early literacy programs is combined with a bilingual script, a sample program, lists of Spanish music to use in your program, suggestions of books for reading aloud, and templates for ten essential flannel board pieces and how to use them. In addition, written guidelines are provided to help you create and maintain a good working relationship with your partner.

Part III, "Personalizing Mother Goose on the Loose en Español," features two chapters that will help you make the program your own.

Chapter 11, "Planning and Customizing Programs and Weekly Activities," offers the best tools to shape a unique program or series of programs. It also provides information and programming sheets to help you create an ongoing Mother Goose on the Loose en Español series for your own institution. It features weekly activities that can be used to familiarize non-English-speaking families with public library services. These include reference questions to ask at the information desk, tours of specific areas, library card registration, book check-out, and hands-on computer demonstrations.

Chapter 12, "Feedback, Evaluation, and Celebration," provides tools for in-house evaluations specifically designed for this program. Questions for the evaluations are in both English and Spanish. Also included is advice about challenging situations with parents and children, suggestions for celebrating successes, and ways to expand your program.

Part IV, "The Mother Goose on the Loose en Español Songbook, Rhymebook, and Resourcebook," contains two chapters. Chapter 13 provides a list of suggested songs and rhymes that work well in this program. The chapter features songs, lyrics, words to rhymes, and stage directions according to section classification (e.g., Rhymes and Reads or Standing-Up Rhymes). Chapter 14 includes developmental tips in both Spanish and English.

Part V, "A Personal Word," includes Chapter 15, "Final Thoughts," which discusses additional resources and the rewards one can experience from this program.

How to Use the CD-ROM

Audio: The CD-ROM contains one complete program to use as an instructional tool. Songs, rhymes, and developmental tips in Spanish, as well as best practices for helping children improve school readiness, are included. The CD also provides parents with activities that they can try at home. Songs and rhymes included on the CD are indicated in the text by the symbol ☉ plus track number.

Simply insert the CD into any audio device to listen. The program is presented as follows:

Track #1	Explanation
Track #2	Introduction
Track #3	Welcoming Comments/Bienvenidos
Track #4	Rhymes and Reads/Rimas y lectura
Track #5	Body Rhymes/Rimas del cuerpo
Track #6	Drum Sequence/Sequencia de "rum pum peta"
Track #7	Standing-Up Activities/Actividades al pararse
Track #8	Animals!/¡Animales!
Track #9	Musical Instruments/Instrumentos musicales
Track #10	Scarves/Pañuelos
Track #11	Lullabies/Cancioncitas
Track #12	Interactive Rhymes/Rimas interactivas
Track #13	Closing Section/Despedida

I found it works best if you and your Spanish-speaking partner both listen to the CD together to get an idea of the types of songs that are available in the program. Then, together you can collaborate to determine if parts should be added or omitted.

Graphics and Documents: The CD-ROM also includes downloadable files for the Program Planning Worksheet (Figure 11.1), Sample Program Plan (Figure 11.2), and Song Lyrics and Directions (Chapter 13), as well as digital templates for the flannel board patterns presented in Chapter 10.

To plan your own lesson:

1. Download the desired number of the program planning sheets onto your computer from the CD-ROM. Two versions are included: the Sample Program Plan features a ready-made program outline based on the program described in Chapter 8; the Program Planning Worksheet is a customizable form that you can use to create your own program.
2. The mandatory materials that need to be consistently repeated are already filled into the corresponding blanks of both versions of the planning sheet.
3. In the Sample Program Plan, the suggested materials that I recommend are listed in parentheses; you can opt to use these or replace them with your own choices by filling in the corresponding blanks on the Program Planning Worksheet.
4. The open blanks on the Program Planning Worksheet are for materials that you choose. Fill in the blanks with the songs, rhymes, and stories that you would like to present in your lesson.
5. Add a developmental tip or two to each lesson (examples are provided in Chapter 8's program plan and in Chapter 14), and you have just planned your own Mother Goose on the Loose en Español program!

By following all of the instructions and using all of the tools presented in *Early Literacy Programming en Español*, any librarian (Spanish speaking or not) can succeed in planning and running a Mother Goose on the Loose en Español program.

Acknowledgments

A gigantic thank-you goes to Ellen Riordan, Coordinator of Children's Services at the Enoch Pratt Free Library in Baltimore, Maryland, who brought Anne Calderón and me together and asked us to create a Spanish version of Mother Goose on the Loose. Her foresight and insight into people is unparalleled. Anne has been the idea partner; working with her has been a joy. We have spent hours planning, running programs, evaluating, discussing, singing, dreaming, laughing, and writing. We've shared the same passion for Mother Goose on the Loose en Español, and I am delighted to be able to make our successful model accessible to others.

Thanks goes to Rosa Hernandez for stepping in when Anne began her doctoral studies in Spanish linguistics. Rosa presented the first official Mother Goose on the Loose en Español training workshop with me, recorded songs in Spanish even when her throat was very sore, and introduced me to "La tortuga Tomasa."

Rahel and Jim McClure are the most incredible recording team ever—each trip up to Betsy's Folly studio in New Hampshire was a new and fun adventure. Thanks goes to librarian Iris Cotto, who responded so enthusiastically to our first Mother Goose on the Loose en Español training workshop that I asked her to be one of the voices on the CD. Iris helped coin the phrase "Eschucha y disfruta" and livened things up by insisting on taking photographs with the chickens outside of the recording studio.

Vicky Lyon has remained a close friend even though I once clogged her plumbing with a lobster as a well-intentioned but inconvenient "birthday surprise." She has generously stepped in and volunteered her time, organizational skills, and marketing experience. Because she took care of the "little things," this program was able to grow.

Shelley Quezada, Consultant for the Underserved for the Commonwealth of Massachusetts, has championed Mother Goose on the Loose since she first read about it in a *Public Libraries* article years ago. Because of Shelley's determination to bring MGOL to the Spanish speakers in Massachusetts, Anne and I were inspired to create the first training workshop for them.

To Rosemary Honnold, editor extraordinaire, for helping to organize all of this material in a logical way and for keeping me focused. To Charles Harmon at Neal-Schuman Publishers for encouraging me to write a second book. To Susan Brandt, for her editing help, general assistance, and moral support. What a great assistant! To Anne Betz for her inspirational piece "The (Not-Really) Rocket Science of Flannel-board Pieces: A Guide for Everyone," and to Gilda Martinez for her contribution of a chapter on bilingual language development as well as her enthusiastic help with the Spanish script. Thanks also goes to Gilda Valdes in Florida and Fran Glushakow for their help in the final stages of the book. And to Mike Kouri, my other editor!

To Melissa Da, who became a superb Mother Goose on the Loose presenter while at the Enoch Pratt Free Library and later used it as the framework for teaching Spanish to preschoolers and kindergarten children at the Mt. Washington Elementary School in Baltimore. Melissa's selection of Spanish-language songs from around the world provided some wonderful new material. To Rachel MacNeilly, for sharing her version of a Spanish-language MGOL as well as ideas about the direction the Spanish workshop should take. To Jennifer Bown-Olmedo for her enthusiasm for spreading MGOL to local daycare providers and to Jamie Finley for making the second Mother Goose on the Loose en Español training workshop possible. To my favorite opera singer, Evelio Méndez from Puerto Rico, for creating some new Spanish translations that fit the beat of each rhyme perfectly and for making a long transatlantic flight interesting by singing the songs aloud with me. To Christy Estrovitz for her friendship and guidance in this new territory.

To Maria V. Escovar de Capriles for being an enthusiastic MGOL mom, for supplying Spanish-language children's materials from Venezuela, and for offering to help whenever needed. To Regina Wade for listening to me go on and on about Mother Goose on the Loose en Español and helping with chapter organization while traveling around the country giving MGOL trainings together.

To Celia, my favorite artist and the best sister in the world, for her love as well as her illustration talents. She is extraordinary, and working with her is always a treat.

To Alon, for giving me a story to tell; to Yoella, who patiently (or not-so-patiently) shared a computer with me while she was doing homework and I was working on this book. To Maya, who always gives cheerful encouragement, even while serving in the army overseas, and to Stuart, my partner in life and sympathetic ear.

PART I

Things You Need to Know Before Starting a Mother Goose on the Loose en Español Program

Chapter 1

Learning, Early Literacy, Spanish-Language Considerations, and Mother Goose on the Loose en Español

Learning and Early Literacy

Until the 1990s, most public libraries did not offer programs for children under the age of three. There was very little in the library literature about programming for this age; some libraries would hold special storytimes for two year olds, but, in general, programming for the under-two age group was almost unheard of. With the advance of scientific techniques for studying the brain in noninvasive ways, it became clear that the architecture of the brain is formed in the earliest years, experiences create connections that make learning easier for children as they get older, and social and emotional parts of that experience are just as important as the cognitive learning. As neuroscientists began publicizing their findings, educators began looking at the brain research in the context of what it meant for the learning and development of young children.

In the 1990s, studies were published and research about the brain was translated into language that laypeople could understand. Information regarding the way children learn came from *Meaningful Differences in the Everyday Experience of Young American Children* (Hart and Risley, 1995),[1] where researchers recorded adults speaking to children in their homes and discovered that children living in poverty hear far fewer words than those with affluent parents. The relationships among the number of vocabulary words a child knows when entering kindergarten, the level of success achieved in school, and the ability to hold a well-paying job as an adult were discovered through further studies.

The High/Scope Perry Preschool Project[2] began in the 1960s and followed two groups of at-risk children from the same background; one group was given a high-quality preschool experience and the other was not. These children are now adults over the age of 40, and the continuing study has shown that the children who participated in the High/Scope preschool have markedly higher rates of a stable family life, steady employment and earnings, and education and significantly lower rates of incarceration.[3] These results have led to the conclusion that there is a clear financial benefit for investing in early childhood education.

In 1994, other research produced data that were taken out of context and used to support questionable practices. According to the idea of "the Mozart effect," listening to Mozart improved a baby's brain capacity. Because politicians and lawmakers wanted children to become smarter, they passed laws in Georgia and Tennessee ensuring that mothers of every newborn American citizen would be given CDs and/or tapes of classical music. State-subsidized child care centers in other states were required by law to play classical music for a certain amount of time each week. Later research showed that the effect of listening to Mozart was only temporary, but, by then, other companies had jumped on the bandwagon and began producing books, videos, and CDs that purported to help young children become smarter by listening to specific music. Flash cards and other tools were marketed to help children learn how to read and count well before the kindergarten years. Some parents believed that the best thing they could do for their children was to expose them to as much material as possible; this overabundance of academic preparation added stress to the lives of both parents and children.

To counter this, in 1997, Daniel Goleman published *Emotional Intelligence: Why It Can Matter More Than IQ*.[4] Other books, such as *Scientist in the Crib: What Early Learning Tells Us about the Mind* (Gopnik, Meltzoff, and Kuhl, 2000),[5] used research to show children as young scientists who create hypotheses and spend their early years experimenting to prove or disprove them. The importance and interaction of significant adults who help facilitate the children's exploration was described. In 2000, *From Neurons to Neighborhoods: The Science of Early Childhood Development* (Shonkoff and Phillips, eds.)[6] tackled the question of nature vs. nurture and used evidence from studies to show that positive personal experiences with caregiving adults was just as important as the surrounding environment. Dr. Shonkoff later used scientific findings to convince public policy makers to fund early childhood programs that focused on the whole child rather than on building academic skills. The importance of positive emotional connections and experiences in the early years was emphasized through papers published by Shonkoff with the National Scientific Council on the Developing Child, asserting that "Young Children Develop in an Environment of Relationships" (Working Paper #1), "Children's Emotional Development Is Built into the Architecture of Their Brain" (Working Paper #2), "Excessive Stress Disrupts the Architecture of the Developing Brain" (Working Paper #3), "The Timing and Quality of Early Experiences Combine to Shape Brain Architecture" (Working Paper #5), and "Mental

Health Problems in Early Childhood Can Impair Learning and Behavior for Life" (Working Paper #6).[7] Stress-free childhoods that included loving relationships with caregiving adults seemed to be the best predictor of academic success.

Einstein Never Used Flashcards: How Our Children Really Learn—And Why They Need to Learn More and Memorize Less (Hirsh-Pasek, Golinkoff, and Eyer, 2003)[8] used research to encourage parents to spend more time with their children, playing with them, singing with them, and exploring the world together in a joyful way. The authors' interpretation of the research suggested that it is better *not* to focus on building academic skills in the youngest years; rather, joyful and imaginative play that follows a child's interest combined with a secure relationship with an adult will help young children build lifelong skills, such as knowing how to get along with others, solving problems, and paying attention, essential for being successful in the world.

Research seemed to be saying that children from birth to the age of three who receive the right kind of stimulation in nurturing environments have a much better chance of doing well in school and in adult life than children who lack this grounding. In the late 1990s, with this as the backdrop, library directors began encouraging their children's librarians to offer programs for the very young, even though there was little literature and practically no traditional library programming for infants and toddlers.

In the middle of this emphasis on child development through interactions with a caring adult, Mother Goose on the Loose stood as a time-tested program that took into account the holistic child and incorporated a philosophy and activities that were sound practices reflecting the findings in brain research related to child development. Mother Goose on the Loose allowed a child to be a child; it did not involve rigorous academic drilling. Yet the children who attended Mother Goose on the Loose programs came away with heightened attention spans and an increased vocabulary; they developed social skills, pre-reading skills, a positive attitude toward learning, and much more. It filled a void in the world of children's programming and was received by the library community with open arms.

By incorporating the music theories of Barbara Cass-Beggs and letting children be children, this program spread throughout U.S. public libraries. Librarians found it was popular, amazingly effective, simple to learn, and very easy to present weekly. All five earliest domains of school readiness (language and literacy, health and physical well-being, social and emotional development, general knowledge, and positive approaches to learning) were incorporated into Mother Goose on the Loose. Language development, including book reading behavior, increased vocabulary, pointing out and naming objects, sound awareness, and recognizing word patterns, was combined with songs and rhymes that seamlessly mixed book illustrations, musical instruments, and activities that promoted positive reinforcement. The early literacy development in Mother Goose on the Loose did not just involve language; it also involved social skills and emotional development, such as learning how to wait patiently, follow directions, and take turns; it helped build each child's self-esteem, and it gave children the opportunity to learn how to appreciate and celebrate the achievements of others. Because it helps to develop multiple aspects of a child's personality and skills in a holistic fashion, Mother Goose on the Loose is richer in content than most other early childhood programs.

The first Mother Goose on the Loose sessions took place in Jerusalem, Israel. It brought together families from different backgrounds in a joyful setting; English speakers, Hebrew speakers, Arabic speakers, and Russian speakers attended Mother Goose on the Loose programs on a regular basis. Singing English-language songs and clapping for each other's children created a warm, community atmosphere; in a country with high political tensions, Mother Goose on the Loose was one place where everyone was friends. Although the majority of parents bringing their young children were from English-speaking countries and wanted to help reinforce the English that was being spoken at home, non-English speakers brought their children in order for them to learn English! By coming on a weekly basis, these children did indeed learn how to respond to directions in English and to answer simple questions. The power of repeated exposure to nursery rhymes in a nurturing atmosphere was evident.

After Mother Goose on the Loose came to the United States in the late 1990s, some librarians began to wonder if the program could be adapted into other languages. Around the country, librarians with large immigrant populations began experimenting with alternative language versions of Mother Goose on the Loose. Because of its flexibility, they were able to keep to the format of 10 sections with 80 percent repetition but would substitute their own translations for some of Barbara Cass-Beggs' songs or replace them with traditional folk songs in the language of their community members.

According to the U.S. Census Bureau, by 2007, there were 45.5 million Latinos living in the United States, comprising 15.1 percent of the population (U.S. Census Bureau, 2008).[9] In 2009, there were more than 32 million Spanish-speaking people in the United States. Public libraries increased collections of Spanish-language materials, began using bilingual signage, and often had official library documents (such as library card applications) available in languages other than English. In addition to materials, libraries wanted to provide programs as well. But many public libraries did not have Spanish-speaking staff and thus were unable to offer Spanish-language programs. The collaboration between the Enoch Pratt Free Library and the Maryland Committee for Children is very important for this reason.

About Nursery Rhymes and Spanish-Language Considerations

There is a direct correlation between knowing nursery rhymes before starting kindergarten and being successful at reading and spelling. The "rhyme-to-reading path" sensitizes children to the sounds in words, and this phonemic awareness helps them learn to read.[10] Some studies infer that early exposure to rhyme and alliteration is a stronger indicator of positive performance at school than actual letter knowledge.[11] Familiarity with nursery rhymes can be more important to a child's success in school than differences in social, economic, or parental educational backgrounds. Because of this, a nursery rhyme program is the ideal format for an early childhood program in the library.

However, many traditional rhymes, in both English and Spanish, are either rooted in gruesome historical events or relate inappropriate expectations and/or behavior. For example, the English nursery rhyme "Ring around the Rosie" dates back to the Black Plague in Europe. It refers to the custom of putting posies in one's pocket to ward off the plague. "Ashes, ashes" refers to the religious "ashes to ashes, dust to dust" that priests recited at the funerals, and "we all fall down" meant that many people died. "Mambrú Went to War," a Spanish song from Bolivia, also tells about death. In the song, Mambrú dies and is taken to his grave, where a little bird is singing.

Negative stereotyping is also present in a number of rhymes. In some versions of "Tortillitas para mamá," Mama gets the nice ones and Papa gets the burnt ones; in other versions Mama is glad but Papa is mad. Because this rhyme is popular and fun, poetic license can be used to simply change a word or two, making the rhyme much more positive. "Pin Pon," a popular song about a boy doll, is sung by Spanish speakers around the world. Some versions uphold Pin Pon as an example to follow because he does not cry when his hair is pulled and he is able to eat his soup without spilling one single drop. It is unrealistic, however, to expect children under two to refrain from crying or to be so well-coordinated that they never spill any soup. To prevent parents from expressing unrealistic behavioral expectations of their children, these verses can be left out of the song. It is important to think very carefully about the messages being sent to children and parents when singing a song. Through early childhood programming, librarians have the chance to positively impact many lives. Because parents look up to the program presenters as models for appropriate behavior as far as child care and child rearing is concerned, it is important to be careful with every action taken and every word sung.

The original Buena Casa, Buena Brasa program did not include many "traditional" Spanish nursery rhymes. Not every song was conducive to exciting/interesting hand motions/movement in the same way as songs by Barbara Cass-Beggs. Only songs that had a totally positive message for children were included. However, it did contain a sampling of traditional Spanish children's songs, such as "Un elefante," "Chocolate," "Los pollitos dicen," "Martinillo," "El juego chirimbolo," and a modified version of "Pin Pon." We also incorporated many translations of English songs that were catchy, well-received, and had great hand movements.

It is almost impossible to include only authentic material in programs, because "authentic" varies according to the region. "Authentic" cultural songs for someone from Argentina are totally different from "authentic" cultural songs for someone from Mexico. Mother Goose on the Loose en Español uses a sampling of appropriate traditional songs supplemented with tried-and-true songs from Mother Goose on the Loose. Because Spanish speakers come from several countries and many of them immigrate to the United States for new opportunities, it is important to show respect and represent the Latino culture through your choice of songs. At the same time, be sure to find ways to introduce your audience to American concepts as well through song.

A difficulty with using "traditional" Spanish rhymes is that, just like the Spanish language, the rhymes vary according to the country and geographic region. For example, "Chocolate" is a very traditional song in some countries, but people in other countries have never heard of it. In addition, the Spanish used across Latin America and Spain varies greatly from country to country and *even within countries*. For example, linguistic empirical studies have shown that Portuguese from Portugal and Spanish from Spain (two different languages) are more similar than Spanish from Spain and some Latin American Spanish. The same is true with English; English-speaking people from different social classes and educational levels have different dialects. In addition, most people speak at least a few registers (formal Spanish, academic Spanish, colloquial ["street"] Spanish, family Spanish, etc.). There are three main ways that this great variation manifests itself: in the lexicon (vocabulary), in the syntax (grammar), and in the phonology (sounds).

Many speakers believe that certain dialects of Spanish are "official" or the most "proper" or "correct." However, there is *no one correct dialect of Spanish*. The Real Academia Española (Royal Academy of Spanish) publishes volumes on Spanish grammar that is generally accepted as the academic norm; however, nobody actually speaks it. Many people may claim that they speak it, or people from such-and-such a country speak the best Spanish, but that is a myth.

How does this relate to what we do at the library? We are not there to criticize the way anyone speaks or to encourage anyone to speak a certain way. Many immigrants come to this country with little education and low self-esteem, believing that the Spanish they speak is somehow inferior to more formal registers or dialects of the upper classes. By using the Spanish that we know and with which we are most comfortable, we are showing them that all dialects are valid and to be respected. If we limited ourselves to providing lyrics in "Puerto Rican Spanish" or "Mexican Spanish," we would be leaving out many other countries. In addition, a native speaker from Mexico with a university education in the Spanish language would still speak differently than people in other parts of the country.

The Spanish used in translating the songs for Mother Goose on the Loose en Español does not come from one particular dialect. Although Anne studied and lived in Puerto Rico, the Spanish used in her translations is not "Puerto Rican Spanish." Anne is a linguist and therefore took many factors into consideration when translating, such as grammar use according to the Real Academia Española and vocabulary that would be either universally inoffensive or the most common variant for the majority of speakers. In her translations, Anne also tried to fit the right number of syllables into each song while still maintaining the original tune. These are the songs and rhymes used in this book.

A few people assisted in the recording of the Spanish script. Each time new people sang a song from the text, they changed it slightly to fit with the way *they* would sing it to their children. Accents differed, tunes varied slightly, and even words changed. Thus there may be some recorded songs that do not exactly match with the written lyrics. This directly illustrates the wide range of interpretation within the varieties of Spanish languages. Using the script as a baseline, the community partners should also be able to use the script as a blueprint for forming a 30-minute plan of their own.

No matter which Spanish is used, non-English-speaking parents and caregivers may question the value of an early literacy program in Spanish. They wonder if they should be speaking Spanish at all to their young children, if they want to help lay the groundwork for their children's success in an English-language environment. These concerns are addressed in the next chapter.

Notes

1. Hart, Betty, and Todd R. Risley. 1995. *Meaningful Differences in the Everyday Experience of Young American Children.* Baltimore, MD: Paul H. Brooks.

2. Schweinhart, L.J., J. Montie, Z. Xiang, W.S. Barnett, C.R. Belfield, and M. Nores. 2005. *Lifetime Effects: The High/Scope Perry Preschool Study through Age 40.* Monographs of the High/Scope Educational Research Foundation, 14. Ypsilanti, MI: High/Scope Press.

3. The findings are summarized at www.highscope.org/Content.asp?ContentId=219 (accessed October 14, 2009).

4. Goleman, Daniel. 1997. *Emotional Intelligence: Why It Can Matter More Than IQ.* New York: Bantam.

5. Gopnik, Alison, Andrew N. Meltzoff, and Patricia K. Kuhl. 2000. *The Scientist in the Crib: What Early Learning Tells Us about the Mind.* New York: Harper Paperbacks.

6. Shonkoff, J.P. and D. Phillips, eds. 2000. *From Neurons to Neighborhoods: The Science of Early Childhood Development.* Committee on Integrating the Science of Early Childhood Development. Washington, DC: National Academies Press.

7. National Scientific Council on the Developing Child Working Papers. 2007. Available: www.developingchild.net/pubs/wp.html (accessed October 6, 2009).

8. Hirsh-Pasek, Kathy, Roberta Michnick Golinkoff, and Diane Eyer. 2003. *Einstein Never Used Flashcards: How Our Children Really Learn—And Why They Need to Play More and Memorize Less.* Emmaus, PA: Rodale.

9. U.S. Census Bureau. 2008. "U.S. Hispanic Population Surpasses 45 Million." Washington, DC: Public Information Office. Available: www.census.gov/Press-Release/www/releases/archives/population/011910.html (accessed October 6, 2009).

10. Bryant, P.E., M. MacLean, L.L. Bradley, and J. Crossland. 1990. "Rhyme and Alliteration, Phoneme Detection, and Learning to Read." *Developmental Psychology*, 26, no. 3: 429–438.

11. Maclean, Morag, Peter Bryant, and Lynette Bradley. 1987. "Rhymes, Nursery Rhymes, and Reading in Early Childhood." *Merrill-Palmer Quarterly*, 33, no. 3: 225–281.

Chapter 2

Bilingual Language Development

Gilda Martinez

Should we teach two languages simultaneously or work on one language first and then work on the second language later on? It depends on who you ask. However, advocates for bilingual language development all agree that being bilingual is advantageous.

Let us begin with parents who speak only one language, such as Spanish. They will speak to, read to, and have conversations with their children in their native language, and the children will develop language and literacy skills in that one language. Once the children enter school, they will be able to transfer those language skills when learning a second language; and, the more the first language is developed, the easier it will be for them to learn a second language. (This is called *sequential bilingualism*.)

Some think this might be confusing because learning a second language is very different from learning a first language, but this is not the case. There are some differences and some similarities. A first language is usually learned at home by young children to communicate to loved ones as an unconscious process and without much time pressure. Children must learn developmental concepts as well as vocabulary. For example, children learn that a bottle can contain milk, juice, or water and quenches their thirst while at the same time acquiring the vocabulary to ask for different types of drinks. A child learning a second language will already understand the concept of a bottle and different types of beverages but will need to learn the terminology in the new language. Hence, skills learned in a first language transfer to a second language, and the more a child has developed a language (any language) the easier it will be to learn a new language. Of course there are times that children will learn new concepts at the same time as learning the second language, but many basic concepts will already have been learned if parents or caregivers spent much time dialoguing in the first language.

Many times parents are not sure if they should raise their children bilingual or if it would be better to just teach them English because that is the language most spoken in the United States. The following excerpt on this topic from Catherine Snow, Professor of Education from the Harvard Graduate School of Education in Cambridge, Massachusetts, summarizes her views on this issue:

> In the early years, Spanish speaking parents should speak only Spanish at home and read to children in Spanish because it is more likely that children will retain Spanish if they have literacy skills in Spanish. The skills the children develop in Spanish will transfer in school to English skills. Parents should also give their children a lot of opportunities to write without insisting that they spell everything correctly. They should also read a lot of rhymes and alphabet books in Spanish. In addition, having many conversations and going to places—the zoo, shopping, children's programs, etc. are generally good procedures to engage in because it gives children access to a rich language environment and helps build vocabulary.[1]

Having a rich oral language vocabulary helps when learning to read, because the child will already know the words they are asked to learn to read (in that language). Transferring the skills to another language will be easier than starting from scratch.

Nonie K. Lesaux, Assistant Professor of Education also from the Harvard Graduate School of Education in Cambridge, Massachusetts, states:

> We can start by promoting language development that is not language specific. Children need to hear a lot of language and play with language. If the language spoken in the house is Spanish, it would be better if they hear it spoken often. A mistake some parents make is that they want their children to learn English so they don't talk to their children often. They should speak to them in Spanish. Children also need lots of print activities to gain an understanding of print and its connection to language to promote native language development. By having one language developed well, it helps literacy acquisition in a second language.[2]

Based on their research, talking, reading, and writing often in the native language seems to work well when beginning bilingual language development if parents can speak only one language. Creating opportunities for children to dialogue, by visiting places or engaging in fun learning activities, are positive ways to begin. Singing is also recommended, even though one may not be an avid singer. (Reading outweighs watching television or DVDs to develop a language because of the wide range of vocabulary used in books and the text connections made, which are not part of the television experience.)

Sequential Bilingualism versus Simultaneous Bilingualism

If both parents are bilingual, how can they teach their child both languages at once (called *simultaneous bilingualism*)? One way is by having each parent choose one language to focus on when speaking with their child. In this way the child learns both languages with less confusion. For example, the mother speaks to the child only in Spanish, and the father speaks only in English. Even though it might take the child longer to become as proficient in two languages as a child learning only one language, the benefits of learning two languages at a slower pace offsets learning a single language at a time. It is also important for parents to know that while children are becoming bilingual it is normal for them to mix the two languages. Code switching, or changing languages while mid-sentence, may simply be a word-finding issue or trying to figure out a word to use if the language does not have a direct translation for the word. Despite this, if two languages are used in the early years, the transition to school will be easier for a Spanish-speaking child with a foundation in English than for Spanish-speaking child who does not speak English.

Some bilingual parents decide to use sequential bilingualism and will teach their child their native language first. However, because young children are very capable of learning two languages simultaneously, and not knowing any English would make the transition to school more difficult, it is recommended that bilingual parents use simultaneous bilingualism to teach their children two languages at once.

Conclusion

Regardless of the sequence chosen, children should learn to speak in the language spoken at home well in order to develop the general language skills necessary to succeed in the beginning years of school. The more they know in any language when they enter school, the greater the chances are they will succeed academically. In summary, developing language through dialogue—talking, reading, rhyming, and singing—while engaging in motivating activities are fine ways to begin on a positive note.

References and Resources for Educators, Parents, and Community Members in English and Spanish

Center for Applied Linguistics (CAL). 2009. Available: www.cal.org. Type "bilingual development" into the search engine to find articles, guides, Web sites, conferences, listservs, and various other research-based documents on the subject.

Childhood Bilingualism: Current Status and Future Directions: www.nichd.nih.gov/publications/pubs/upload/Childhood-Bilingualism_2005.pdf. This 38-page document summarizes a workshop on this topic provided by the U.S. Department of Education, the U.S. Department of Health and Human Services, the American Federation of Teachers, the American Speech-Language-Hearing Association, and the International Reading Association.

Colorin' Colorado: www.colorincolorado.org. This Web site includes videos, information, activities, and advice for parents (and educators) about bilingualism and how to help their children succeed in school.

Help My Child Read: Reading Tips for Parents: www.ed.gov/parents/read/resources/readingtips/index .html. This free online book helps parents get their children ready to read and learn, describes how to spot a good early reading program, and provides simple strategies for creating strong readers.

Helping Your Child Become a Reader: Available: www.ed.gov/parents/academic/help/reader/index.html. You can also download this book for free or order a free copy. It provides developmentally appropriate activities for children from infancy through age six. It is available in Spanish and English and shares information on reading, learning about books, and reading in other languages.

How to Help Your Child During Preschool Years: With Activities for Children from Birth to Five: www.ed.gov/espanol/parents/academic/preescolar/index.html. This free book provides techniques for parents to develop school readiness skills while keeping learning motivating and fun. Activities and information focus on children five and under.

National Association of Bilingual Education: www.nabe.org. Information about promoting bilingual education, the importance of fostering a multilingual society, programs, and research are a few of the many topics addressed on this Web site.

Prepare My Child for School: Healthy Start, Grow Smart Series: www.ed.gov/parents/earlychild/ready/healthystart/index.html. First Lady Laura Bush initiated this series of booklets, which can be downloaded or ordered for free. They contain information about raising children from birth to one year and descriptions of what to expect each month during the first year.

Reading Rockets: Launching Young Readers: Available: www.readingrockets.org. This Web site provides information about teaching children to read and how to help those who struggle. Current videos, articles, news, and views from around the world are available with one click, as well as major findings in literacy research and bilingual development.

What Works: Promising Practices for Improving the School Readiness of English Language Learners: www.aecf.org/upload/publicationfiles/ec3655k762.pdf. You can download this e-book for free. It provides examples of strategies and practices that have been used to improve the school readiness of English Language Learners, as well as bilingual development research. Tips for Educators, Parents, and Caregivers in English and Spanish are also provided.

Notes

1. Martinez, G., and A. McMahon. 2004. *What Works: Promising Practices for Improving the School Readiness of English Language Learners.* Baltimore, MD: Ready at Five Partnership.

2. Ibid.

About the Author

Dr. Gilda Martinez is currently a faculty member in the Department of Educational Technology and Literacy in the Graduate Reading Program at Towson University. Her work involves researching pre-kindergarten English for Speakers of Other Languages (ESOL) students' literacy progress in south Florida; researching the successes of college students from urban areas throughout the United States who received a scholarship through the Ron Brown Scholar Program; serving in various university, state, and national organizations; and teaching graduate reading courses, including an ESOL course she developed for teachers working on their Master's in Education-Reading who wish to attain ESOL certification.

As a reading specialist, she has taught several graduate level reading courses at the Johns Hopkins University, Loyola College in Maryland, and Towson University. She created and advised for the ESOL graduate programs at Johns Hopkins. She also provided technical assistance (e.g., with curriculum development, program evaluation, grant writing, and coaching) and professional development support to administrators, teachers, child care providers, parents, and librarians throughout the nation.

She has presented at various state, national, and international conferences on topics such as best practices in early literacy instruction, ESOL reading and writing strategies, mentoring beginning teachers, team building, and creating homeschooling connections. She has also published articles in *School Community Journal, Internet Teachers of English as a Second Language (TESL) Journal, Education Review, Reflections Journal,* and *Children and Libraries* and co-authored the book *What Works? Promising Practices for Improving the School Readiness of English Language Learners.* She is fluent in Spanish and enjoys providing workshops to parents in her native language.

Chapter 3

Working with the Latino Community

Anne Calderón

Finding a Cultural Partner

Librarians interested in facilitating a Mother Goose on the Loose (MGOL) en Español program at the library, regardless of their background, should seek a cultural partner as a first step. Finding a cultural partner to share programming responsibilities is an excellent way to establish the in-roads necessary for community acceptance. A cultural partner is a staff member of a local service-based organization who is either a member of the same ethnic group as the intended library program participants or very familiar with the culture. This person works in conjunction with the librarian assigned to the program; while the children's librarian has expertise in children's programming and literacy, the partner offers cultural knowledge and a link to the community. It is also desirable that the cultural partner have some knowledge of child development, education, or a related field. In other words, the sole act of speaking native Spanish does not guarantee that the cultural partner will be sensitive to the needs of young children and families.

The library can find a cultural partner by investigating community resources. Many cities have some type of Latino service provider group that acts as a forum for professionals from all fields who provide direct services to Spanish speakers. There are several ways that the library facilitator can find a group of this type. First, he or she can use an Internet search engine and enter keywords such as "Latino community organizations" plus the name of the city or geographical region. Also, call local service organizations that help Latinos. The library facilitator can ask to speak with a client representative or a community worker and question him or her regarding how professional service community news is relayed and whether there is a professional organization of service workers in the area.

To quickly disseminate information, attend a Latino service provider meeting and make an announcement about library programs and the search for a cultural partner. Nonprofit, family-oriented organizations are also prime candidates for a cultural partner and often share similar missions and goals with those of the MGOL en Español program. The librarian may also check with local university extension programs, community religious organizations, and child care training organizations.

Once the library has found a cultural partner, it is important to establish a positive and mutually beneficial relationship. The next step is to find common interests and identify goals. Also, the library and cultural partner should be clear regarding funding and the number of work hours each party will spend on MGOL en Español. If one party is working with a grant, be sure that all grant requirements are met. In order to achieve this, it is sometimes necessary to change small components of the program. In addition, it is crucial to always use a contract or memorandum of understanding between the library and the cultural partner. The library should identify one specific contact person for the cultural partner (this may be the MGOL en Español librarian or it may be a supervisor). Last of all, the library and cultural partner should meet regularly for updates to address concerns and celebrate successes.

There are some cases in which working with a cultural partner is not entirely necessary or not an option. For example, a children's librarian wishing to facilitate MGOL en Español who is already an active Latino community member may not need a cultural partner. In this case, the librarian can skip the first step of finding a cultural partner.

Reaching the Latino Audience

A common roadblock encountered by libraries reaching out to Spanish speakers is getting new patrons into the library. After considerable effort and few results, many libraries give up trying to attract Latinos. A different approach, however, is all it takes to integrate new Spanish-speaking patrons into library programming. Many libraries depend solely on a library newsletter and Internet site to advertise programming. While these means will attract middle-class, English-speaking patrons, they seldom reach all sectors of the Latino community. Working-class immigrants are not as likely to have Internet access or to be computer literate; therefore, other methods need to be employed to reach this community. Affluent Spanish speakers may prefer to read Spanish papers and view Spanish-language Web sites. In-house library advertising would most likely not reach this group either.

Finding and Attracting Program Participants

Fliers in Spanish advertising the library and library programming are helpful to hand out along with a personal introduction. Social service workers can distribute these fliers at events that library staff are not able to attend. It is advisable to refrain from relying solely on fliers and news advertisements to spread the word. Although fliers are an effective way to advertise when used to supplement a conversation or an introduction, by themselves they lack the personal touch that often piques people's interest.

Even though the addition of a cultural partner eases the process of finding participants from the community, it is still necessary for the librarian and the cultural partner to go into the community and meet with possible participants. The staff working on this task can start by investigating service organizations in the area that provide assistance to Spanish speakers. Health care clinics, family involvement and immigrant rights organizations, domestic violence prevention programs, and the previously mentioned Latino service provider organizations are all good places to start to reach the immigrant population. The librarian and cultural partner can visit these organizations and make arrangements to attend meetings, events, and community functions during which Spanish speakers will be present. An effort should be made on the part of the library staff to be approachable and friendly, informally chatting with Spanish speakers before and after these events.

Head Start and pre-kindergarten programs provide a wealth of possible participants. Cultural events, such as Spanish language film festivals and Hispanic Heritage Celebrations, restaurants serving food from Central or South America, and clubs that feature Latin music can be good places to advertise upcoming programs for Spanish-speaking parents. In addition to following the above suggestions, library staff may arrange to conduct a shortened version of the normal MGOL en Español during a parent meeting or parent visiting hour at one of these early education programs. A quality sampling of interactive songs and rhymes that focus on the children's many abilities is sure to encourage Spanish speakers to attend library programming. Regardless of the exact method used, the library program is most likely to grow steadily once a few loyal participants and patrons are established. These participants are an essential link to the rest of the community and will readily spread the word if they are satisfied with library services.

Welcoming the Latino Audience to the Library

The library space should generally be welcoming and accommodating so that participants feel comfortable from the moment they enter. Alongside a display of English books should be a display of Spanish books, reminding participants that the library also has materials in Spanish. A simple sign in Spanish may be placed at the circulation desk indicating that library card applications are available in Spanish. It is also helpful to label library collections in both English and Spanish. A simple addition such as a sign saying "Libros en Español" will direct patrons to materials with which they are most comfortable working. If possible, place Spanish materials in an easy-to-find area or leave a Spanish sign near the entrance directing patrons to the Spanish collections. The Texas State Library has an excellent Web site (www.tsl.state.tx.us/ld/projects/bilingualsign/childrens.html) that provides basic phrases for signage in Spanish.

While ideally every library would have at least one staff member who speaks Spanish, this is seldom the reality. However, there are still many steps that any library can take to ensure that Spanish speakers are able to receive the services and help that they need. In addition to appropriate signage indicating the availability of library cards and the locations of Spanish collections, be sure to have library card applications available in Spanish. A list of frequently asked questions translated to Spanish can substitute for a verbal explanation of library card policy and be used by the circulation staff. Another effective tool for distribution is a laminated wallet-sized card with useful phrases in English and Spanish, such as, "I need a book about ___" or "I want to renew this."

The Spanish in Our Libraries (SOL) Web site at www.sol-plus.net/plus/home.htm provides extensive resources including simple phrases in Spanish that librarians may want to use, library forms and documents in Spanish, press releases and a library glossary. The Webjunction Web site also addresses library services for Spanish speakers. An English/Spanish guide for frontline library staff, conversation guides, and a vocabulary list for librarians are among the helpful resources (available at www.webjunction.org/spanish-for-staff/resources/wjarticles).

Expectations of Library Staff

Although it is not expected, or realistic, that all staff take Spanish classes, a staff member with even limited Spanish proficiency may lead staff in a ten-minute Spanish session during a staff meeting. This short session should teach basic greetings, such as "Buenos días" and "¡Hola!" For more serious learners motivated to brush up on high school Spanish or gain experience in the language, several libraries may join together in offering a six- or eight-session class on Spanish basics for librarians. Regardless of the proficiency level, staff who are comfortable doing so should be encouraged to use a simple Spanish greeting with Latino patrons. But never forget that the most effective and welcoming greeting is a genuine smile! A smile is guaranteed to make anyone feel welcome. Considering that the circulation desk is often the first place where library visitors have contact with library staff, it is of the utmost importance that the circulation staff be friendly and welcoming.

If there are security guards at your library, be sure to introduce them to program participants at the very first session. Because program attendees may be fearful of adults wearing police or security uniforms, explain that they are stationed in the library to keep everyone safe. Asking a guard to say a few welcoming words in Spanish will help in alleviating fears.

Accommodating the Latino Parenting Style

The MGOL en Español facilitator should be aware of several cultural differences while planning programming. The facilitator may find it useful to share some of these cultural considerations with general library staff in order to best prepare everyone involved. Every culture has distinct ways of child rearing and different concepts of community. Although forming stereotypes is harmful in multiple ways, there are some overlying generalizations that may be helpful to keep in mind.

Many Latinos have a great sense of the importance of community in child rearing. Just as the phrase "it takes a village" has been applied countless times in child rearing, Latino parents often count on other community adults to assist in gently disciplining and generally watching over their children. This shared responsibility becomes even more pronounced within an established group of acquaintances. The library staff, however, should never have to discipline children. If this becomes necessary, the MGOL facilitator should have a conversation with the parent of the child, explaining gently that the parent needs to take a greater responsibility toward the child's behavior. Frequent occurrences of this type should also be addressed to the entire group in the form of a "public service" talk. The facilitator should never recount the challenging event or share names; rather, he or she may share information with the parents, framing the talk as a parenting tip.

Along these lines, many Latino parents have a more relaxed view of the child's independence. Latino parents often allow their young ones to wander around on their own, without following closely behind or holding their hand. For example, a Latino mother waiting for an MGOL session to start may let her two year old walk around the children's department by himself while she chats with other parents. This may make the library staff nervous, being unaccustomed to seeing children exploring the environment by themselves. Note that there exists a fine line between cultural sensitivity and responsibility for a child's safety. While the library staff should recognize and respect different parenting styles, they also need to ensure a safe environment for children, and it certainly is not solely the staff's responsibility to do so.

To address this issue, the MGOL facilitator may wish to add an additional opening remark for the parents present. The facilitator can explain that while staff understand and appreciate children's curious natures, parents need to keep their children within eyesight. The facilitator should give an example of this, referring to actual library space, to help parents understand the limits. "We understand that children need to explore their environment and be independent. While we encourage this, we also ask you to please keep your child within eyesight. For example, if you are here in our programming space talking with other adults and you can no longer see your child, you must stop your conversation and look for him. He may have wandered off to the circulation desk. If he is not in this area, you must get him and bring him back."

Educational methodology has made great advances in the past decades and has helped to create inclusive and warm learning environments. However, many of today's adults, independent of country of origin, had negative experiences as children in the educational system. They attended elementary school during a time when educators set unrealistic goals for young children and when teachers were to be feared. This strict and unaccommodating educational environment was often a harsh reality for today's Latino adults. In Latin American countries of years past, parents handed all responsibility for a child's education over the teacher, including the use of physical punishment. It was very common for teachers to criticize and embarrass students in front of the entire class. Children were expected to remain totally silent unless called upon by the teacher, in which case they were to stand up at the side of their chair and provide the required information. Unfortunately, there was little room for creativity or independent thought and belief on the part of the children.

All of these experiences are highly likely to influence both the behavior of adult participants in Spanish MGOL programs and the expectations they have of their young children. Parents attending MGOL programs may view the facilitators as flawless and all-knowing. The library facilitators should not be surprised if adult participants call them "maestro" or "profesor" ("teacher" or "professor") and generally maintain social distance from them. Various useful techniques in breaking these barriers include an invitation on the part of the facilitators to address them by their first names or "Miss Anne" or "Mr. Bob," for example. In addition, before and after the program the facilitators can initiate conversations about neutral topics with adult participants, such as inquiring about cultural traditions in the home country. However, the best way to establish a bond with parents is over the child. The facilitators may ask about likes and dislikes of the child or comment on a positive development milestone they noticed. Even simply asking, "What new thing has your child done this past week?" is a good way to open communication with the parents.

Developing trust is a slow process that must be handled with tact and sensitivity. Once program participants trust the library facilitator and staff, they are more likely to become part of the library community. They will then begin to encourage other ethnic community members to go to the library. The many suggestions given throughout this book will help to create a library environment that lends itself to building trust.

Other Considerations

One additional point to be put into practice regards the issue of immigration status. Library staff should never inquire about the immigration status of patrons and program participants. The library is a neutral and accepting institution that welcomes all people, regardless of immigration status. Many undocumented immigrants are cautious, and sometimes even frightened, to leave their homes and participate in the wider community due to fear of deportation. Any hint of a discussion regarding immigration status in the library is enough to keep many people from ever returning. On the other hand, the library staff should find ways to satisfy the domestic and identity requirements necessary for the attainment of a library card for those who are sensitive to immigration status. If not, the library risks alienating parts of the Latino community.

In order to make the application for a library card nonthreatening for the non-English speaker, some libraries give people applying for library cards a blank postcard to fill out. They address the postcard to themselves, and the library mails it out. When the postcard arrives at its destination, the person who wanted a library card brings the postcard back to the library. The postmark is a legal stamp and the fact that it was delivered to the person at his or her stated address establishes a bona fide place of residence. This is an unobtrusive method for determining residency, and a library card can now be issued.

In some cases, the facilitator is the only American English speaker with whom the Spanish-speaking parents have contact and have established trust. Once this confidence is established, the program facilitator should take advantage of this relationship to provide them with links to community resources that offer assistance to immigrants. In particular, immigrants will welcome information on food banks, English classes, Head Start programs, computer classes, and health resources.

About the Author

Anne Calderón, originally from Chicago, has facilitated Mother Goose on the Loose en Español since its inception in October 2006. Her favorite part of the program is seeing the sense of community that develops among participants. She obtained her degree in Spanish Linguistics at the University of Illinois at Urbana–Champaign, during which period she had the opportunity to spend time studying and living in Puerto Rico and Brazil. After spending two years in Baltimore developing early childhood development and early literacy trainings for Spanish speakers, Anne is now working on a PhD in Second Language Acquisition at Georgetown University.

PART II

Planning for Mother Goose on the Loose en Español

Chapter 4

Guidelines for You and Your Partner

How to Prepare with Your Partner

You have now found someone in the Spanish-speaking community who is very enthusiastic about working with you to present programs to Spanish-speaking families. But you can't just start running programs immediately, because your partner has never worked with children or run programs in a public library before. Although it is essential to have a Spanish speaker to help present your program, you must also insist on offering a high-quality program in the public library. Therefore, before you can even start planning your Spanish-language programs it is important for you to work with your partner to show him or her what you would like your end result to be. Start by describing your ideal early-childhood program. Invite your partner to observe a few of your Mother Goose on the Loose programs. Show her the *Mother Goose on the Loose* manual (published by Neal-Schuman, 2006) or the weekly program plans that you have saved on your computer.

Explain that Mother Goose on the Loose en Español follows many of the principals of the English-language Mother Goose on the Loose program:

1. Repeating 80 percent of the material from program to program
2. Including one or two developmental tips in each program
3. Using some songs written or adapted by Barbara Cass-Beggs
4. Following the ten-section structure, in order

To familiarize your partner with the program you want to create and present together, talk about each of these components. Take a careful look at the ten sections, giving examples of the activities in each section and then mentioning a skill that the activity promotes (see the next chapter for more information on this).

Once your partner is familiar with the entire program, go through the sample program song by song and decide which songs you want to keep and which you want to replace (see the Program Planning Worksheet and Sample Program Plan in Chapter

11 and on the CD-ROM). Do you want to keep any of the songs in English? If so, which ones? Do you want to have an entire section in English?

An easy way to do this is to photocopy or print the Program Planning Worksheet and Sample Program Plan to use as your guides for planning your own program.

- Ask your partner to fill in some Spanish-language rhymes in some of the sections.
- Decide which Barbara Cass-Beggs rhymes you would like to keep in English and which you would like to use in Spanish. Write the titles of the rhymes in the appropriate places.
- Ask your partner if there is something she wants to add into the program. Decide together if is developmentally appropriate, and, if so, write it in.

Consider the Spanish-language songs you have chosen. If some of them are English songs translated into Spanish, check with your partner to see if the Spanish used will be familiar to the majority of your families. Your partner may want to consider substituting traditional Spanish-language songs from the country of origin of your local families in place of the some of these songs.

This is fine. However, be sure to get an English translation of any new Spanish song added or substituted. Just as traditional nursery rhymes sometimes need to be tweaked to avoid violence or sexism (Georgie Porgy Pudding and Pie kissed the girls and made them cry, the old woman who lived in the shoe whipped all her children soundly, or Peter Pumpkin Eater imprisoned his wife in a pumpkin shell), traditional Spanish rhymes may seem to be innocuous but may upon second glance be giving out a message that is not developmentally appropriate. (Refer to the section "About Nursery Rhymes and Spanish-Language Considerations" in Chapter 1 for more information.) After working together in this way to create your first program, you should have a list with the majority of the rhymes in Spanish and some in English.

When Anne and I did our first programs together, the animal section was only in English, and I led that part of the program. The adults who came loved having that exposure to English. Anne wrote the words in English on posters, and during the animal section we displayed the posters. The adults enjoyed being able to sing along in English, and they rapidly learned the English names for the animals as well as the sounds they made. Because I did not speak any Spanish, this gave me direct time with the group, which helped them feel connected with me as well as with Anne.

Look at your Program Planning Worksheet again. Write out a "script" that includes full lyrics for all of the rhymes that will be used by both you and your partner.

- Assign a leader for each rhyme and activity. Make sure that you lead at least three rhymes in English.

- Practice running through the program together. Listen carefully to the rhymes in Spanish and try to recite them softly along with the leader, even if you can't say them perfectly.
- Gather any relevant props for the rhymes, and see if you can create movements to jazz up some of the more sedate ones.
- Invite a colleague or two to watch a practice run-through, point out the things that work best, and offer suggestions for improvement.
- If you know Spanish speakers, invite them to watch a run-through and share comments and suggestions.

Review your written program and have one more practice session with another colleague. When you feel ready, start advertising for your first program!

Advertising the Program

Write an advertising blurb with your partner that includes a short description of the program. Be sure to mention refreshments, times of the program, ages of the children targeted, and contact phone number of the partner for questions and transportation information, and highlight the fact that the program is free. This blurb should then be translated into Spanish. Your partner can advertise it in Spanish through her organization; you may want to use both the English and Spanish versions to publicize the program in your library literature.

Your Continuing Relationship with Your Partner

Questions that need to be answered and recorded in a memo of understanding, to avoid misunderstandings later, include the following:

- Who is going to supply the props (flannel board/easel, musical instruments, puppets, colored scarves, CD player, CDs, etc.)?
- Where will the materials be kept when the program is not taking place?
- Can partners have access to the props when the program is not in session?
- Who is responsible for setting up the room for the program?
- Who is responsible for cleaning up the room after the program?
- Who will pay for the refreshments?
- Who will go to the store to buy the refreshments?
- What should be done with leftover refreshments?
- Who will count the number of participants and keep the statistics?
- How will you evaluate the success of the program?
- When will you meet to reevaluate?

Resolving these issues in advance helps minimize the confusion caused by the odds and ends of the program.

Assessing the Program on a Regular Basis

Even the best laid plans can run into snags. It is useful for you and your partner to plan to meet for at least 30 minutes following the first five programs. There are bound to be problems, and it is worth discussing them immediately after each session. You can brainstorm solutions together, provide a sounding board for each other, and, through open communication, make sure to stay on the same page. Taking notes during these evaluation sessions can be useful. When the program has been running for awhile, you can use these notes to write an article for your local newspaper, to apply for grants, and to show your library administration how this program has made a difference in the lives of the people attending as well as in the number of Spanish speakers using library facilities.

Discussion after the first few sessions might include the following:

- What should we do about the little boy who keeps running down the stairs?
  - Buy a baby gate and install it at the beginning of each program.
- What should we do about the mother who refuses to take her child out of his baby carriage?
  - Be patient, but encourage her to unstrap him and give her positive reinforcement when she does.
- What can we do about the mother who forces her child to sit on her lap?
  - Repeat that "children this age don't sit perfectly still" and "it is fine if a child wants to wander around" at the beginning of each session. If this does not work, speak privately with the mother.
- What can we do about the little boy who always walks up to the bells, pulls them out of the bag, and rings them throughout the program?
  - Find a high shelf near the flannel board where we can store the bag of bells until they are needed.

Because you are a children's librarian and your partner may not be an experienced children's programmer, try to be a tactful mentor:

- Always find something positive to say about the program.
- Ask your partner what she thought about that day's session and listen carefully to her answer.
- Keep in mind that your partner has probably not had storytime training, and there are bound to be things that were not covered in your whirlwind planning sessions. Suggest new ideas tactfully:

- o   Try holding the book in one position rather than moving it around as you read it; you may find that children are able to focus better on the illustrations that way.
- o   Don't forget to add positive words after each child says "Stop" while hitting the drum.
- o   I wonder if that rhyme is a bit too long and confusing for the children.

Do not be a know-it-all, but do participate in a respectful dialogue that will keep your programs top notch.

Preparing for the Program

Providing Transportation

You may decide that the only way to bring participants to the library is to provide transportation. Many non-English speakers find it hard to get out of their neighborhoods and are uncomfortable taking public transportation. Providing transportation to and from the library could make or break attendance at your programs. Of course, funding for transportation must be in place before this can even be considered as an option. However, if funding is available, these are the next steps to consider:

- •   Even if your library provides the funding, your partner should take responsibility for arranging the transportation.
- •   Find a transportation company that values parent–child relationships. Make sure to check references!
  - o   It is very important that drivers greet families in a friendly manner, encourage parents for singing or reading to their children, and reinforce the patterns of behavior that the librarians are promoting.
  - o   Car seats must be provided for children and seat belts for adults.
  - o   Safe driving must be a priority.
  - o   It is not necessary for drivers to speak Spanish as long as they are respectful and friendly.
- •   Decide which areas the transportation will cover.
- •   Let community members know that transportation is available for free but only on a sign-up basis.
- •   Publicize your partner's phone number as the contact person for arranging transportation. Refer all interested participants to her.
- •   Each week, on the day before the program, your partner should call all interested participants and ask if they would like a ride. She will tell them an approximate time to be ready for pickup. She will then submit a list with names and addresses of all families who need rides to the transportation company.

Providing Refreshments

Across cultures, food brings people together. Providing refreshments is an incentive that brings people in the library for the first time. It can provide sustenance for families in low-income households who may not have enough food. It is also a way to educate about nutritious eating, which fosters healthy brain development in children. Also, eating together creates community. Having snack time after each program provides a venue for people to get to talk together informally (with each other and with you!). This is how you get to really know the people attending your programs. Suggested refreshments include the following:

- Fresh seasonal fruit
- Juice boxes with 100 percent juice
- Low-sugar applesauce cups
- A tall pitcher of water with ice
- Cheese squares
- Whole wheat crackers

Occasionally, during snack times you may want to explain that you chose these particular foods because they are healthy and good for children.

Here are some tips for getting your library ready:

- Learn how to say a few welcoming words in Spanish, such as "¡Holá!" and "Buenos días."
- Assess availability of library materials in Spanish and create some if needed, including:
  - Library card applications
  - List of library hours and locations
  - Borrowing policies
  - Directional signs
  - Signage for sections with Spanish books, music, and periodicals
- Speak with the circulation staff ahead of time:
  - Let them know that you are expecting non-English speakers who have not been in the library before.
  - Encourage them to use a welcoming word in Spanish and to have Spanish-language library card applications available.
  - Request their patience, as first time library users often need repeated explanations of procedures.

Know What to Do at Your Very First Program (and at Every Program)

Be friendly! Greet everyone warmly and use a word in Spanish, such as "¡Holá!" Introduce yourself, and ask people for their names and the names of their children.

As you start your first program, ask your partner to translate for you paragraph by paragraph:

- Welcome everyone to the library, and tell them you appreciate their attendance.
- Describe the function of a public library.
- Introduce the library staff.
- Introduce the security guard (if your library has one). Make sure to let your visitors know that the function of the guard is to keep the library safe, and he is there to help. Have the guard say a few welcoming words in Spanish (such as "Buenos días") to help alleviate fears.
- Point out the location of the bathrooms.

Then, set the scene for the program with the welcoming comments and begin the program. Be prepared to spend more time on this program than the official program times; if you are relying on transportation, there are guaranteed to be days when the attendees all arrive late or are kept waiting at the end of the program for the transportation to take them home. Decide your policies ahead of time. If people generally arrive 15 minutes late, will you wait to start the program or always start it on time no matter what? If the transportation is late in picking up the families, where should they wait? Is there a place in the library where they can wait while the children (who have now been in the library for a fair amount of time) can move around? Is there a safe area for them to wait outside? By being prepared in advance and anticipating a variety of scenarios, you will be ready to handle anything once your program begins.

Chapter 5

Supplies

Supplies

To run a basic Mother Goose on the Loose en Español program, you will need some basic supplies. This chapter lists the items along with suggested suppliers. Recommended vendors and Web sites were based on prices and availability at the time this book was written; feel free to do your own Internet search to see if you can find better prices!

The Flannel Board/Easel

The "5-in-1 teacher's easel" flannel board is an easel with a flannel board on one side, a chalkboard or magnetic whiteboard on the other side, and a shelf in the middle of both sides (see Figure 5.1). The flannel board and easel is just the right width for storing flannel characters and some props and books out of the sight and reach of the young children at your program. This is an essential piece of equipment. You can arrange books and flannel board pieces directly on the shelf in the order in which you will be using them. They will not distract the children if they are kept out of sight. Although this easel can be ordered from Brodart (www.brodart.com), it is also carried by many companies. It is worthwhile to check online for the best price before purchasing one. The main producer of these easels seems to be Best-Rite®; try searching the Internet for Best-Rite® Teacher's Easels.

Figure 5.1: 5-in-1 Teacher's Easel

A Chair or Stool to Sit On

Choose a stool or a chair that is unobtrusive but sits you at an easy height for reaching the shelf in the middle of the easel.

Plastic Storage Tub with a Tight-Fitting Cover

A plastic storage tub with a tight-fitting cover is an essential piece of equipment. Although the tub should be relatively large, this tub should be able to fit inside the easel on the floor underneath the inner shelf and should not be made of clear plastic. This kind of storage tub can usually be found at stores such as Target and Kmart.

Flannel Board Pieces

Flannel board pieces that have some connection with the rhymes being recited provide important visual clues to the youngsters. Rather than relying on ready-made pieces, buy flannel or felt pieces from a fabric store and create your own using tacky glue. Flannel board templates for Mother Goose on the Loose en Español are included in Chapter 10 of this book. For high-quality felt finger puppets at good prices that can also be used as flannel board pieces, go to www.artfelt.net. Artfelt offers packages with the rhymes included; for instance, they have "Two Little Blackbirds" with many variations in English and one verse translated into Spanish.

Colored Scarves

Music Rhapsody offers a set of 22 scarves in multiple colors (Item #3009) at www.musicrhapsody.com/store.php4 (see Figure 5.2). To keep the scarves friendly and not scary, the children must be able to see through them, even if they are placed over the children's heads in peek-a-boo fashion.

Figure 5.2: Colored Scarves

Puppets

A few farm animals (puppets or stuffed animals) are necessary for each program. These can be ordered from Folkmanis at www .folkanis.com. Folkmanis puppets look realistic enough to help children learn to correctly identify the animals but are not scary or unwieldy. Although the prices are not the least expensive on the Internet, if you are a public library ordering more than a certain amount, there is a discount. Be sure to talk with the company directly before placing your order. These are some puppets to consider purchasing:

> A turtle for "La tortuga Tomasa"
> An elephant (or two) for "Un elefante se balanceaba"
> One hen for "Los pollitos dicen"
> Additional farm animals such as a cow, a pig, a sheep, a horse, a rooster, or a dog for the Barbara Cass-Beggs' farm animal songs

While spider puppets are great for "The Eency Weency Spider" and "The Great Big Spider," many companies only have scary-looking spiders. Demco sells a very friendly looking spider glove puppet at www.demco .com/goto?BLK6200&LPCK71 (see Figure 5.3). In addition, if you want a smaller spider, try the mini-spider, by Folkmanis.

Percussion Instruments

Percussion instruments for your program include the following:

- A tambourine or a drum
  - A tambourine with a drumhead or an easy-to-carry drum is needed for the Rum Pum Pum Drum Sequence. The "Hand Drum by Remo" or "Sound Shapes" can be purchased from Music Rhapsody at www .musicrhapsody.com/drums.php4 (see Figure 5.4)
- Bells
  - Have enough bells to give one to each child and each adult at your program. Colorful, easy-to-grasp animal bells called "Animal Shaped Bells" can be ordered through Empire Music at www.empire-music .com/US/English/ViewCategory .cfm ?Category=218. They are also called "Easy-Grip Jingle Bells" and can be ordered through Lakeshore Educational at www.lakeshore learning.com/seo/ca|searchResults ~~p|DB952~~.jsp (see Figure 5.5).
  - "Cluster bells" are three bells on a stick that are very easy for even the youngest children to hold. They are available from a variety of stores, including Discount School

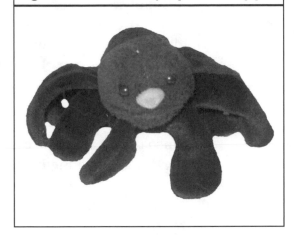

Figure 5.3: Friendly Spider Puppet

Figure 5.4: Tambourine

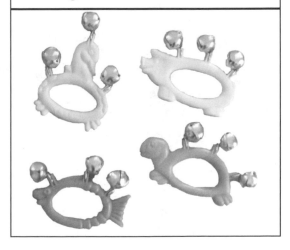

Figure 5.5: Animal Bells

Supply at http://www.discount schoolsupply.com. For newborns, you may also want to try to the "Jingle Bell," an instrument with one bell set at the top of a painted hardwood handle. Sets of six are available from Kaplan Early Learning Company at www .kaplanco.com/store/trans/category ListingRpt.asp (see Figure 5.6).

- Maracas
  - Make sure you have enough maracas to give one to each child and each adult at your program. Do not get the large ones; they are too big and too loud for children under the age of three. Purchase "chikitas" instead. You can find some at Empire Music; they are called LP RhythMix chickitas and are sold in pairs at www.empire-music.com (see Figure 5.7).
- Wooden rhythm sticks
  - When using wooden rhythm sticks, be sure to have enough to give two to each child and each adult at your program. These are often difficult to find. The most common rhythm sticks are much too long for children under the age of three; some sticks that are usually the right length are called "claves" and are quite expensive. The most cost-effective way to buy rhythm sticks is to go the hardware store, buy some dowels, have them cut to size (6 inches is good), and sand them. Or, go to Kimbo Educational's Web site (www.kimboed.com/rhythmsticks .aspx) and purchase their set of 12 pairs of 6-inch rhythm sticks for a reasonable price (see Figure 5.8).

Figure 5.6: Cluster Bells

Figure 5.7: Maracas

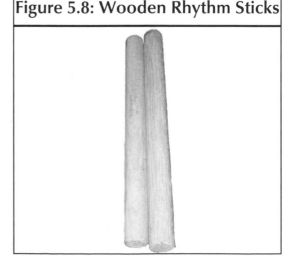

Figure 5.8: Wooden Rhythm Sticks

- Storage containers for musical instruments and scarves
  - Canvas bags, Bongo Buckets, or baskets are great for storing and carrying your instruments, scarves, and puppets. If you are using canvas bags, make sure that they are wide enough for the children to comfortably place their instruments and scarves in when you are walking around the circle collecting them. When not in use, keep the bags in your plastic storage bin or hang them on a coat rack! Mother Goose on the Loose canvas bags can be ordered at www.cafepress .com/mgol .288220978 (see Figure 5.9).

FIGURE 5.9: Canvas Bag

A CD player

To play recorded music, you need a CD player with adequate speakers.

Optional Accessories

Foam Board with Select Spanish/English Lyrics

If you want to stress written language, or if your public has expressed the desire to learn English, you may decide to write out the words to select songs on a large foam board. You can prop up the foam board against the front of the easel when you sing that particular song.

Developmental Tip Cards

If you have difficulty thinking of developmental tips, you may want to use preprinted developmental tip cards. A great resource for this is *The Early Literacy Kit: A Handbook and Tip Cards*, which I wrote with my colleague Saroj Nadkarni Ghoting in 2009. It is available from ALA Editions at www.alastore.ala.org/detail.aspx?ID=2634.

Song Cards

If you need prompts with words for songs and rhymes, a great resource is "The Music Box." This large index box contains lyrics and instructions for 180 well-known rhymes, songs, fingerplays, and activities. Musical notations and available recordings are also listed on these sturdy laminated cards, which can easily fit in between your flannel board pieces on the shelf inside of the easel. It is available at www.elzpublishing .com/index.html. For information about music to use in your program and recommended CDs, see Chapter 9.

Of course, it is fine (and even preferable) to use more props, such as other musical instruments and a candlestick for jumping over. These are not necessary, however, in order to run the basic program.

Books

Books to Use in the Program

Because you will be using some books on a regular basis, keep a copy of each with your programming materials and do not let them circulate (although you should be sure that you have additional copies in your circulating collection). These are some books you can use every week:

> *Los pollitos dicen/The Baby Chicks Sing* by Nancy Abraham Hall and Jill Syverson-Stork and illustrated by Kay Chorao (Little, Brown Young Readers, 1999)
> *Mother Goose Rhyme Time* by Kimberly K. Faurot (Upstart, 2006), which is a nursery rhyme book in English with lovely illustrations and accompanying posters with text and more illustrations
> *Tortillitas para mamá* by Margot C. Griego, Betsy L. Bucks, Sharon S. Gilbert, and Laurel H. Kimball and illustrated by Barbara Cooney (Henry Holt, 1981)
> *The Very Busy Spider* by Eric Carle (Philomel, 1995) or another book with large, colorful illustrations of a variety of farm animals

For information on more good books to read aloud in Mother Goose on the Loose en Español, see Chapter 10.

Resources: The Original Mother Goose on the Loose Manual

If you would like more information about Mother Goose on the Loose, the original manual contains everything you ever wanted to know! *Mother Goose on the Loose: A Handbook and CD-ROM Kit with Scripts, Rhymes, Songs, Flannel-Board Patterns, and Activities for Promoting Early Childhood Development*, written by Betsy Diamant-Cohen and published in 2006 by Neal-Schuman, can be purchased through Neal-Schuman at www.neal-schuman.com/bdetail.php?isbn=1555705367.

Chapter 6

Setup, Structure, and Repetition

Setup

Getting Your Programming Area Ready

If possible, hold your program in a library area that has plenty of room and few distractions. If this is not possible, make sure to move furniture out of the way, cover up computers with paper tablecloths, and use chairs to form moveable barriers or area rugs to define circle-time space.

Mother Goose on the Loose en Español follows a specific structure. The program area should be set up with a flannel board/easel at the front and a stool or chair on either side of the easel for the librarian and cultural partner (or they may both choose to sit on the floor). Place the plastic storage tub underneath the easel shelf. Put Bongo Buckets, bags with musical instruments, animals, and scarves behind the easel or on a shelf directly behind the easel, where little hands can't reach them. Place your flannel board pieces and books (with pages marked by sticky notes) in the order in which they should be used in the storage bin, and make sure the cover is on tightly!

Having the pieces you will use on the flannel board close by makes your job much easier. Flannel board pieces that represent a rhyme or activity also serve as a reminder of the rhyme that comes next while you are actually presenting your program. To keep the program running smoothly, it is recommended to make a pile of all the materials in the order in which they will be used and to place them on the shelf inside of the easel. Sticky notes should be placed in books with illustrations that match particular rhymes. These books, the relevant flannel board pieces, cards with developmental tips, and notes with any other information should be stacked on the shelf in the order in which they will be used. Then, the piece staring you in the face will be your reminder of the activity to do next.

If you are inviting children to play afterward, fill a plastic storage tub with educational toys, fasten the cover securely, and put it in an unobtrusive place in your storytime area that is close enough for you to bring out as soon as the program has finished. Have a few easy puzzles or toys on the floor before the program starts to keep early visitors occupied. Before starting your program, gather up the toys (singing the clean-up song). Ask everyone to sit in a semicircle around the flannel board with the children on their parents' laps, facing you.

When you are ready to begin the program, take the flannel board pieces and books out of the storage bin and place them on the shelf inside of the flannel board easel, keeping them in order. Put other props on the far side of the shelf. Place the CD player where curious children who like to press buttons cannot touch it but not too far away from the facilitator. Load the CD player with the music selected for the day, and put it in the PAUSE mode. You are now ready to start presenting the program.

If you plan on doing weekly surveys, be sure to have your pencils, clipboards, and papers set aside in the program area where they are easily accessible but out of the reach of little hands. If you are serving refreshments after the program, be sure to have enough plates, cups, napkins, and tableware (if needed). Wash all fruit ahead of time, cut anything that needs to be cut, remove plastic wrapping that is unnecessary, pour a large pitcher of water, and place crackers on plates. Put anything that needs refrigeration in the refrigerator, and cover up everything else with a paper tablecloth. Keep these items out of sight on a book truck that can be wheeled into the room when needed, or set them on a table in another room that can be locked while you are presenting the program. Be sure to have a sponge on hand for wiping the tables and a large garbage can with a liner by the door.

Structure

Each program should have ten segments, which generally stay the same from week to week. The segments are thoroughly described in Chapter 7. They are used in the following sequence:

1. Welcoming Comments/Bienvenidos
2. Opening Rhymes and Reads/Rimas y lectura
3. Body Rhymes/Rimas del cuerpo
4. Rum Pum Pum Drum Sequence/Sequencia de "rum pum peta"
5. Standing-Up Activities/Actividades al pararse
6. Animals!/¡Animales!
7. Musical Instruments and Props/Instrumentos musicales y accesorios
8. Lullabies/Cancioncitas
9. Interactive Rhymes/Rimas interactivas
10. Closing Section/Despedida

Repetition

Eighty percent (yes, that's right!) of each program should remain the same from session to session. This means you will be often reciting the same rhymes and using the same props. However, there must still be variety in each session, even though 80 percent of the rhymes and activities remain the same from week to week. Variety can come in many different forms.

For instance, the rhyme "Un elefante se balanceaba" might be used in each session. However, the facilitator might use different ways to present the rhyme, such as moving a stuffed animal elephant to act out the motions, showing an illustration of the rhyme from a book of Spanish rhymes, showing an illustration of an elephant from an English-language picture book such as *Elmer* by David McKee (HarperCollins, 1989), showing a photograph of an elephant from a nonfiction book, or putting various flannel board pieces relating to the rhyme on the easel.

A few rhymes and songs can be changed from week to week as another form of variety. Singing "Un elefante se balanceaba" at one session might be substituted with "Los pollitos dicen" for the next session. "Los pollitos" might be repeated for the next two or three sessions. Then "Un elefante se balanceaba" can be revived in place of "Los pollitos," or it can be substituted for one of the other rhymes.

Although only one book is read cover to cover in each session, the same principle of repetition applies. The facilitator can choose to read a different book at each session as part of the 20 percent change from time to time, or she may choose to repeat the same book, or she may choose to vary the way the book is read—perhaps reading the book aloud in Spanish one week, singing it the next, and then reading it aloud in English another week. In other words, the library facilitator should feel no pressure to procure a new and exciting example of children's literature every week. By staying in tune to children's interests and likes, the library facilitator can judge the needs of the groups as far as story repetition and variation are concerned.

Use of musical instruments can also add variety. Playing the same instruments from session to session is fine if a few of the songs and activities that accompany the instructions are rotated. However, another way to vary the selection is to substitute different musical instruments. For instance, if bells are generally used, a substitution of maracas will add variety. The maracas can be played for a few weeks, and then the bells can be returned. Alternatively, you may choose to introduce rhythm sticks for the next few sessions and then finally return to the bells. A quick rule of thumb for the 80 percent repetition is to change about five to seven things from session to session!

Extra Tips for Running the Program

Families may bring older siblings as well to attend your programs. To prevent boredom, pull the siblings aside before the program starts and introduce them to one of your stuffed animals. Explain that the animal really wants to participate in the program but does not have a parent to sit with. Ask the children if they will act as the parent for the animal, bouncing it on their lap, holding it, and rocking it when needed. This often ensures an attentive and willing older child participant for your program! In addition, because babies and young children love watching and imitating older children, their enthusiastic participation can enhance the program.

During your program, try to keep instructions to a minimum. The program lasts for only 30 minutes, so don't waste time announcing what will happen next—just do it! Instead of saying, "Start with two fists in front for this rhyme," just start doing the finger play. By watching you, your audience will figure out what to do. Not only does this save time, but it also promotes active listening! Use the same technique throughout your program; chant or sing instructions while demonstrating the action you are looking for. Using a clean-up song to make collecting instruments into a game rather than a chore is a good way to close the program and clean up in the process.

Chapter 7

The Ten Sections Explained

1. Welcoming Comments/Bienvenidos

Welcoming participants in Spanish to the current session of Mother Goose on the Loose (MGOL) en Español is a great way to help people feel comfortable and reassure them that they are in the right place. The immediate use of Spanish also reinforces that this is the primary language spoken throughout the program. The content of the Welcoming Comments is the same as in the English MGOL programs; however, it is even more important to address the parent and child expectations due to those cultural differences in participation previously discussed.

Each MGOL en Español session *must* start with Welcoming Comments that include an introduction, an explanation, and a defining of boundaries. This information helps to create the optimal learning environment:

- Introduce yourself, welcome everyone to the library, and invite them to check out materials after the program.
- You may want to mention some of the benefits of the program: aids speech development and motor coordination, develops attention span, provides exposure to musical instruments, and encourages a love of books and book illustration.

How it works:

- All rhymes will be repeated twice. If you already know the rhyme, say it twice with me. If you don't know it, listen the first time and repeat it the second time.

Set the ground rules for the program:

- Clearly state that "Children this age do not sit perfectly still, and it's fine if they want to wander around."

- Explain that children standing directly in front of the flannel board can block the view of everyone else. Also, if a child comes up and takes one of the puppets or musical instruments from behind the flannel board and starts to play with it, other children will want to come up and take props too.
- Therefore, tell parents to pretend there is an invisible semicircle around the flannel board and that if their child comes within this semicircle, please come up and physically take them back to sit in your lap.
- Also remind parents that while library staff understand and appreciate the curious nature of children, parents need to keep their children within eyesight. Refer to the actual library space to help parents understand the limits. You may want to say something like, "We understand that children need to explore their environment and be independent. While we encourage this, we also ask you to please keep your child within eyesight. For example, if you are here in our programming space talking with other adults and you can no longer see your child, you must stop your conversation and look for him or her. Your child may have wandered off to the circulation desk, but if he or she is not in this area, you need to go get your child."

Mention guidelines:

- All cell phones must be turned off. Children will get the most out of this program if they see that you are fully engaged. So, turn off your phones, and please sing with gusto and enthusiasm.
- If your child begins to scream or cry, please take him or her out of the program area until he or she calms down. Then feel free to come back in.
- Children learn by imitating their parents and caregivers. When you participate with enthusiasm, they will be inspired to join in the activities and to become fully engaged.

Some parents do not know what typical behavior is for a young child. They think a child is supposed to sit still and listen to everything even if the child is only 9 to 14 months old. If their children get up and walk around inside of the circle, the parents may get embarrassed. By giving this brief introduction, parents learn that it is normal for their children to move around and that this behavior is not disrespectful or unacceptable. At the same time, boundaries and rules are established. By telling parents in advance to physically pick up their children and bring them back to the circle if they come within a certain distance of the flannel board, you are reinforcing the fact that such behavior on the part of the children is not unusual and letting the parents know what they are expected to do in such a case.

Without this direction, parents might feel physically conscious of their bodies and may be embarrassed to get up in front of everyone to remove their children from the flannel board area. They worry about interrupting the session and wonder if it looks like they are physically abusing their children. Hearing the rules ahead of time provides parents with reassurance regarding the normality of their child's behavior *as well as* having clear instructions regarding the acceptable/expected/desired response. Verbalizing your wishes for the way you hope those situations will be handled sets the scene for a relaxed program in a warm, nurturing environment where children are allowed to act like children and where parents are confident in responding to their children's actions.

When everything is clearly spelled out, parents can put their attention into the program itself instead of self-consciously wondering about how to deal with their children's behavior. The children will sense this ease in their parents and integrate it into themselves. The librarian will not need to interrupt to give the parents instructions and will not have to direct children away from the props in the middle of the program. It is a win-win situation for all.

Recap

Welcoming Comments/Bienvenidos sets the tone for a comfortable place:

- Leaders introduce themselves.
- "Children will be children."
- Set boundaries with invisible semicircle.
- Come and get children if they come within invisible semicircle.
- Please turn off cell phones.
- If your children cry, leave and come back when they are calm.
- All rhymes will be repeated twice.

2. Opening Rhymes and Reads/Rimas y lectura

This opening section lasts for about five minutes and is the quiet time of the program. This is when the children are most attentive and can sit still for the longest. It is a time to help expand their vocabulary and to expose them to book illustrations.

The opening rhyme should always be "Estamos contentos." This signifies the beginning of the program, signals that it will be an MGOL en Español program, and gives the children a sense of security because it is repeated from week to week. Following this are songs and rhymes with fingerplays or movements that are often accompanied by picture book illustrations, flannel board pieces, props, or puppets. This opening section should last for no longer than five minutes. If you see the babies getting restless, start moving into the body rhymes because they are more interactive than the Opening Rhymes and Reads.

Some time during this opening section, read a picture book aloud. When planning a program for children under the age of two, it is best to choose a very short picture book with colorful pictures and minimal text. This is the only time during the entire program that a book is read aloud from cover to cover, so make sure it is just right for your audience. Pop-up books or books with flaps (like the Spot[1] or Maisy[2] books), books written in rhyme, large board books, and books with photographs of interest to little children (such as of babies' faces) provide good choices. If a story is a bit too long, skip over pages to keep it short and interesting to the children.

Read in an enthusiastic and happy manner. You are modeling book-reading behavior to the parents by showing them that they do need to be able to read proficiently in order to share books with their children. By using books in a joyous way, the children will absorb the happy feeling related to books and carry it on later in life—one of the values that is now associated with school readiness! You are also showing the parents what types of books are best for reading to very young children. Remind participants that they can check the books out of the library when they leave the program.

The facilitator should take special care in choosing and reading the book during the Opening Rhymes and Reads section. In addition to normal considerations necessary for choosing books to read aloud to very young children, one must take into consideration the language of the selection, the level of English of a possible English-language selection, the quality of the Spanish or bilingual book, and the age appropriateness of the book.

Unless the MGOL en Español program is to be totally in Spanish, the facilitator may wish to introduce small amounts of English by means of reading English-language books during the Opening Rhymes and Reads section. This exposure to English has many benefits for both parents and children. First, it begins to prepare children for the English immersion once they start preschool or kindergarten. They will enter school with a head start if they are already familiar with processing English sounds and even possibly interacting with a storyteller in English. Second, hearing English-language books will familiarize Latino parents with simple English vocabulary in a non-threatening environment. While the facilitator reads the book, parents can interact with their children and encourage appropriate responses by following the lead of the facilitator. After all, adults learn another language in much the same way children do: through exposure, interaction, and the repetition that is so common in children's literature.

A good option regarding book language is to alternate weekly between English and Spanish selections. Regardless of the language, however, occasional repetition among titles is highly encouraged.

If choosing an English-language book to read during the Opening Rhymes and Reads, the facilitator must be sure that it is appropriate for English-language learners. Even though many of the same factors come into play when choosing an English book as when choosing a Spanish book, there are a few special considerations. First, avoid English-language books that have silly or make-believe words. English-language learners need concrete examples of conversational and written English. For example, some Dr. Seuss books, while exceptional children's literature in many regards, contain many "nonsense" and made-up words. Beginning English-language learners will not yet have the language skills necessary to see the humor in such literary devices and recognize that they are not actual words in the English language. Second, the facilitator should seek English books that contain high-frequency content words, much repetition, familiar concepts (animals, routines), and clear sequencing. This will enable children and adults to benefit the most from each reading selection.

With the Latino consumer market growing at unheard-of rates, Spanish and English–Spanish bilingual children's books can now be found easily at most local bookstores. The MGOL en Español facilitator, however, should not simply reach for the first book with a Spanish title without carefully considering the quality of the book and the translation. While an in-depth discussion of the characteristics of quality children's literature is outside the scope of this book, there are nevertheless key points to keep in mind that refer specifically to selecting high-quality Spanish and bilingual children's books. These are covered in Chapter 10.

Recap

Opening Rhymes and Reads/Rimas y lectura is the quiet time of the program, and its key components include the following:

- General rhymes
- Interesting book illustrations
- Flannel board characters
- One book read cover to cover

3. Body Rhymes/Rimas del cuerpo

Following Barbara Cass-Beggs' structure for Your Baby Needs Music classes, the third section involves body activities. It should last about five minutes. Start at the head and work your way down the body. Name body parts as you interact with them so that children will learn terms for parts of their anatomy as well as words for those parts' functions. From the head, move down to the hands and fingers. Songs that involve clapping hands, rolling wrists, moving fingers, and waving can all be considered hand songs. This is a good time to insert whole-body songs such as "Can You Kick with Two Feet?"/"¿Puedes patear con dos pies?" or "The Eency Weency Spider"/"La araña pequeñita."

From there you can move to the belly with a tickle rhyme or go straight down to the legs. Knee bounces are great fun. Give directions to the parents so that they know exactly what to do: "Put your legs out straight in front of you. Put your child on your legs facing me. Gently bounce your legs up and down."/"Ponga sus piernas derecho delante de usted. Tome a su hijo en las piernas para que los dos estén mirando en la misma dirección. Suavemente muevan las piernas para arriba y para abajo."

Because children love bouncing movements, they rarely get bored in this section. Children who have started wandering around often come back to sit on their parent's lap for this part. So don't do just one knee bounce. Do two or three! Children love variations of speed and height in rhymes, such as "This Is the Way the Ladies Ride"/"Así a caballo," when the speed and type of bounce varies according to who is doing the riding in the song. This is a fun place to add an English-language knee bounce; try the delightful leaning motions of "Mother and Father and Uncle John."

Recap

Body Rhymes/Rimas del cuerpo involves body activities:

- Start at the head and work your way down the body.
- Encourage positive physical contact between adult and child.
- Knee bounces are one of the most popular activities.

4. Rum Pum Pum Drum Sequence/Sequencia de "rum pum peta"

Section four contains an activity that will lead to standing up. Take a small drum or tambourine and tap it while saying "Rum pum peta, escucha mi pandereta" (Rum pum pum, this is my drum). Continue with, "Me llamo ___, ¿y tú?" (My name is ___, What's your name?) Make sure to tap out the appropriate syllables on the drum while you are saying your name. Because phonological awareness is one of the language skills leading to school readiness, recognition of syllables in this way can be very important. Often, parents will not understand about tapping out the syllables—they may not even be able to hear the syllables as you tap them out. Therefore, demonstrate what you mean when you tell them to tap out the syllables in their names: Juan (one tap) or Rosario (three taps: Ro-sa-rio). Repeat these instructions with the examples *every time*. Be aware that syllables in Spanish are not always the same as in English. For instance, the name "Sylvia" in English is pronounced with three syllables: Syl-vi-a, but in Spanish it is only pronounced with two syllables: "Syl-vya." Eventually, the parents and children who seem not to be hearing the syllables will begin to recognize them and then will become able to tap their own names in syllabic form.

Then walk around the circle asking each child to tap out his or her name by syllables on the drum. After each name, be sure to welcome the child with a personal comment such as "Hola," "Buenos días," or "Mucho gusto." Smile and look each child in the eye as you give your own verbal greeting. Once everyone has tapped their names, tap on the drum as you recite "Párense todos" (Everyone, stand up).

Recap

The Rum Pum Pum Drum Sequence/Sequencia de "rum pum peta" is important for the following reasons:

- It builds a personal connection between the leader and each child.
- It personalizes the program for each child.
- It encourages phonological awareness.

5. Standing-Up Activities/Actividades al pararse (and Positive Reinforcement)

By now, the children may be getting a bit restless, so having some stand-up rhymes and movement helps them to shake their wiggles out. In this section, everyone stands up in a circle and moves to various rhymes for about five minutes. Some traditional Spanish-language songs work very well in this section. "El juego chrimbolo" uses rhythm and body parts to bring participants closer together into a tighter circle. "Bate, bate, chocolate" encourages concentration by requiring a clap on each syllable of the word "cho-co-la-te" after counting to three in Spanish. In the second part of the rhyme, children love the contrast of lowering their voices while squatting down and then jumping up and shouting out the last "¡chocolate!"

Freeze games are fun and useful because they teach children the word "stop." One rhyme in particular is easy to recite and can involve a number of vocabulary words. "And We Walk"/"Y caminamos" requires everyone simply to walk around in a circle, to turn, and then to stop. Substituting other words such as "run," "march," "creep," "tip-toe," "jog," and "jump" is a great way to teach vocabulary. Actually doing the named action at the same time as reciting the corresponding English or Spanish word is a wonderful way to reinforce its meaning. If you want to use this section to also help strengthen English vocabulary, Barbara Cass-Beggs has a great song to the tune of "The Farmer in the Dell." The words are simple: "We're marching to the drum, we're marching to the drum, hi-ho-the derri-o, we're marching to the drum." Everyone marches in a circle to three verses of this song until the song's end when "The drum says *stop*." At this point, walk around the circle asking each child, "Can you hit *stop*?" and hold out the drum for them to hit. If the children are too young to hit the drum on their own, encourage their parents to use the child's hand to hit stop on the drum. As they hit stop, say something encouraging. Sing this song two more times. Each time, vary the movement to the drum; for instance, instead of marching use creeping, jumping, running, galloping, hopping, spinning, sliding, and tiptoeing. Lyrics to this song are on page 146.

In addition to increasing vocabulary, this is a great time to model positive reinforcement. As the children hit the drum, encourage them by using words such as "good," "great," "wonderful," "fantastic," "terrific," etc. You will see the smiles that spread over their faces as they are complimented for doing what they were asked. You are also modeling behavior of giving positive reinforcement for the parents and giving them the vocabulary to use.

These are positive words in English:

Good	Extraordinary
Very good	Awesome
Good job	Incredible
Great	Unbelievable
Excellent	Marvelous
Fantastic	Magnificent
Fabulous	Wonderful
Terrific	Splendid
Tremendous	Superb

These are positive words in Spanish:

Bueno	Fabuluso
Muy bien	Estupendo
Magnifico	Maravilloso
Fantástico	Fenómeno

Once everyone is standing up, you may want to add in some stretching rhymes. "Head, Shoulders, Knees, and Toes"/"Cabeza, hombros, rodillas y pies" is especially good if you have a large crowd or are in a small space where movement is not easy. If your group consists of babies, parents will carry the babies around with them as they perform the activities. If the children have started walking, they will delight in doing all of the actions on their own.

In this section, you can also play some recorded Latin American music, hand out maracas, and have everyone dance. It's a great way to move to the beat, hear music from different Spanish-speaking countries, have fun together as a group, and shake off excess energy. When it is time for everyone to sit back down again, use a rhyme such as "Handy Spandy" or one of the Spanish rhymes to turn sitting down into a game.

Recap

Standing-Up Activities/Actividades al pararse has several functions:

- By the middle of the program, exercise is needed.
- Using freeze games teaches the word "stop."
- Naming different types of movements can expand vocabulary.
- Asking a child to hit "stop" provides a great opportunity for modeling positive reinforcement.
- After expending energy, children can sit for awhile longer.

6. Animals!/¡Animales!

This is the optimal time to use book illustrations. Because everyone is tired from the standing-up exercises, they find it easy to look and listen. Matching sounds to visual representations is a pre-reading skill; here children see animal illustrations and sing out the sound that each animal makes. Eric Carle's *The Very Busy Spider* (Philomel, 1995) has wonderful, large, and colorful illustrations. Children never tire of seeing these pictures—you can use the same book during this part of the program every week for one or two years, and children will continuously enjoy seeing their animal friends and describing the sounds they make. Barbara Cass-Beggs' song, "I Went to Visit the Farm" goes well with the illustrations. School readiness skills of enthusiasm for books and general knowledge about the world are strengthened in this section.

Sometimes, animals from different countries make different sounds. Thus, it is important to be consistent with this activity; if you are going to sing the song in English, make the appropriate sounds to go along with each animal. If you are going to sing the song in Spanish, make sure you know the sounds used by your particular community, and use those.

This activity models using books joyfully with children without actually reading. Adults who are unable to read or who are uncomfortable with traditional reading can learn through example how to "read" pictures with young children. If the librarian is doing it, then it is clearly okay for them to do it also! After participating in this activity for weeks, a person who does not speak a word of English may choose to check out a copy of *The Very Busy Spider* because she will be familiar with the book and know exactly how she can use it with her child. They can sing animal songs, name the animal, describe the animal, talk about where they might have seen the animal, make up stories about the animal, etc. You may want to ask your Spanish-speaking partner to use this activity to promote a positive use of books with children while not necessarily reading them. A few developmental tips could point out the value of this type of playful interaction with books.

At the end of this song, the children may start getting restless again. A good distraction now is puppets. A big duffle bag or deep canvas bag can be brought out at this time, and a guessing game with animal sounds begins. An easy English-language song is Barbara Cass-Beggs' "When the [Cats] Get Up in the Morning, They Always Say [Meow]," and this has been translated into Spanish. However, there are many other animal songs that can be used. "Old MacDonald" can be a bit long, so if you use it, sing only a few verses. Some of the traditional Spanish-language songs about animals are "Debajo de un botón," "La araña pequeñita," and "Los pollitos dicen."

Sometimes children will want to come up and take the stuffed animals, so, as you finish singing about each particular animal, drop it into the plastic tub. The tub should be either behind you or inside of the flannel board/easel where little hands will not be able to get at it. This is when the instructions you gave at the beginning of the program really come in handy!

Next, launch straight into the rhyme "Hickory Dickory Dare." A Spanish version of this song is included on the accompanying CD, or you may decide to create your own. This particular rhyme gives each child the opportunity to throw a puppet up into the air and receive applause for following instructions. After reciting the rhyme once, explain that you are going to pass the stuffed animal around the circle and give each child a chance to throw it up in the air. Remind parents that if their children are too little to toss the stuffed animal up into the air by themselves that they can help by taking the children's hands into their own and tossing it up together. Tell everyone to applaud after each effort to show appreciation for a job well done. Then walk around the circle, giving the animal to each child. As they throw the animal up in the air, recite one of the positive English or Spanish words and applaud. If you have a large crowd, you may decide to do this activity with your Spanish-speaking partner. Your partner can start with the first child sitting next to the flannel board on one side of the circle and work his or her way around while doing the activity in Spanish; you can start with the first child sitting next to your side of the flannel board and work your way around the circle leading the activity in English. End the activity when you both meet in the middle of the circle! As you applaud each child's efforts, encourage the adults to follow your lead. After just a few weeks, even the very youngest children will try to throw the animal up in the air in order to receive positive feedback.

Older children also enjoy this activity. They usually like to throw the animal up higher and appreciate your noticing their skill. A compliment about this skill usually is rewarded with a big smile from the older child.

Once you return to your seat, repeat the rhyme one more time as you throw the animal in the air and catch it. Then put it in the tub, and begin your next activity.

Recap

Animals!/¡Animales! has several advantages:

- You can model how to use a book joyfully without actually reading it.
- Young children find it easy to learn animal sounds.
- Children build self-confidence by correctly recalling and reciting the animal sounds.
- Puppets grab the attention of most children.
- Controlled puppet throwing provides another opportunity for positive reinforcement.

7. Musical Instruments and Props/Instrumentos musicales y accesorios

When you have finished with the animals, go straight into using the musical instruments and/or props. Children may be getting squirmy (they have been involved in the program for quite a long time already), and, by playing an instrument, you will easily recapture their attention. Music stimulates their senses of discovery and scientific inquiry by giving them an instrument to explore: What does this do if I shake it? How does it feel? How does it taste? What else can I do with this instrument? Walk around the circle carrying a canvas bag full of instruments and hand an instrument directly to each child and each adult. This section should last about five minutes from distribution to collection of instruments.

Once everyone has a musical instrument, begin singing a variation of Cass-Beggs' "We Hit the Floor Together." Sing out the name of the instrument and the way it is played, for instance: "We ring our bells together," "We tap our sticks together," or "We shake our rattles together." Translations for all of these songs are provided in Chapter 13. Following the introductory song immediately are instructions: "Shake them *up high*, shake them *down low*, shake them in the *middle*." "Up high" should be sung in a high voice, "down low" in a very low tone, and "in the middle" in your regular tone of voice. The words "high," "low," and "middle" will be easy for the children to learn because they are using movements that correlate to the meaning as they verbalize the word. Again, a Spanish translation for this is provided in Chapter 13. Adding a variation in tone of voice increases the learning to include more than one meaning of the words high and low—"high" is experienced as a tone as well as a physical space, and the same is true for "low" and "middle." And experience is what strengthens brain connections!

Follow this with one or two songs related to what the instrument or prop can do. For instance, ringing and singing "Are You Sleeping, Brother John?"/"Martinillo/Frère Jacques" might be your second activity if using bells; sticks can be tapped in varying tempos to "Grandfather's Clock"/"El reloj de abuelo"; and shaking maracas will help keep the beat when listening to recorded music. Use a variety of music from week to week. In addition to highlighting the wide variety of Spanish music, from salsa to flamenco, you may also want to include classical music, jazz, folk songs, rock and roll, zydeco, bluegrass, and children's songs.

At the end of the session, recite the arriba, abajo, en el medio/high, low, and middle ditty, and walk around the circle with an open canvas bag singing the clean-up song geared for the specific item; if you have just used bells, the song would be "Bells Away." Barbara Cass-Beggs has a very simple clean-up song in English that is a bit more complicated to sing in Spanish. You may want to use this song, which is on the CD recording, or make up one of your own!

As you start circling the crowd, ask parents to give to you all the wet items that have been in the babies' mouths rather than placing them back into the bag. Once the session ends you can sterilize the wet instruments by washing or disinfecting them. If you have time, follow one of these prop sessions with another. Bells can be followed by colored scarves, rhythm sticks can be followed by bells, and bells can be followed by maracas.

If you are using colored scarves, you may want to introduce them with another Barbara Cass-Beggs song, "Wind, Oh Wind"/"Viento." Colored scarves that are translucent do not frighten children if put over their heads, so they are great for playing peek-a-boo. This activity can give you and your partner another opportunity to walk around the circle playing peek-a-boo with each child while playing the song on the accompanying CD. The scarves can also be used for imagination activities—scrunch them into a ball, or use them as washcloths. Perhaps offer a developmental tip for parents who are having a hard time with babies who do not enjoy taking baths: if you turn the activity into a game, the children are more likely to cooperate. Scarves can also be for anything from flowers, to wind, to fish. They are easy to manipulate by waving, blowing, throwing, scrunching, etc. When your audience is composed of children under the age of three, mention the name of each color as you are handing out the scarves. With older children, this is not a good idea because you may encounter children who prefer one color over another!

When it is time to finish, collect the scarves by singing the same clean-up song you sang for the preceding prop (although you may need to substitute "scarves" in place of the name of the musical instrument). There should not be too many activities in this section; two to four per prop is fine. Keep in mind that your entire program should last approximately 30 minutes, so choose your activities accordingly.

Recap

Musical Instruments and Props/Instrumentos musicales y accesorios supports several developmental goals:

- Children are encouraged to explore sounds and textures.
- Children develop listening skills.
- Play and imagination are encouraged.

- Children can be exposed to music from a variety of sources.

8. Lullabies/Cancioncitas

The hustle and bustle of the musical instruments and props can make some children tired, whereas it can rev up the energy level of others. Before moving on to the end of the program, a lullaby at this point helps children to relax while sharing physical closeness with their adult. Although not all children will be prepared to sit quietly rocking with their caregiver, it is a valuable part of the session. Think of the hectic lives we lead as adults and how important it is to learn how to relax and take time to calm down.

Explain to parents that lullabies are most effective when children are snuggled close while singing and rocking. As the children hear the adult's heartbeat and experience the rocking motions, they subconsciously remember the time when they were still in the womb. Incorporating lullabies into your program also teaches parents an effective parenting tool. They may be unfamiliar with the songs and through them will learn techniques for calming down their children. A developmental tip may encourage parents to try using a lullaby to calm their children if they are having a temper tantrum. Some parents may need several reminders that the techniques used in the library program can also be replicated at home.

A lullaby is important for other reasons, too. All children have different internal styles. Some children like lots of excitement, and others prefer quiet times. It is important for the children who thrive on constant movement to have a time when they learn how to sit back and relax. For the quieter children, the lullaby time may give them the energy to finish through the rest of the program.

In MGOL en Español, the lullaby placed at this point serves an additional purpose. The next activity is going to involve each child individually coming up to the flannel board, which may take a bit of time. Young children often find it difficult to be patient and take turns, so the lullaby slows down the pace of the program.

Recap

Lullabies/Cancioncitas have these uses:

- They introduce relaxation techniques that adults can use with children.
- They give children a brief rest period before the grand finale.

9. Interactive Rhymes/Rimas interactivas

As part of the closing section, it is good to include some type of interaction that involves large motor skills. Try placing a candlestick on the floor and reciting "Jack Be Nimble!"/"¡Juan Alerta!" while inviting children to take turns jumping over the candlestick. Remind parents to clap and give positive recognition as each child completes the task. If your group consists mostly of parents with babies, bring the candlestick to them. Walk around the circle, placing the candlestick in front of each adult and infant. Applaud as each adult lifts their child over the candlestick.

"Humpty Dumpty" is another fun activity that is chock full of school readiness skills. Recite "Humpty Dumpty" in English or Spanish as a flannel Humpty sits on his wall, and pull him off as he has "a great fall." Invite all of the children to take turns coming up and pulling Humpty off of the wall. Mention that each child has one turn. Tell the adults that if each child does not go back to his or her seat after taking a turn, traffic jams can form at the front; encourage parents to help their child by physically bringing him or her back to their lap if this should occur. And, ask everyone to clap each time Humpty is pulled off of his wall, so the children will feel appreciated for a job well done.

This type of activity develops a skill called "self-regulation." Instead of having children raise their hands or take turns by going around the circle, the children are asked to monitor themselves. One child will run up to the flannel board the minute he sees Humpty, and another child may wait until everyone has finished before slowly walking up to the flannel board and timidly pulling Humpty off of his wall. Learning how to be patient, to take turns, to follow instructions, to appreciate the achievements of others, and to accept recognition for their own achievements is compounded with the fun of being able to pull something down and to enter into an area (the invisible semicircle around the flannel board) that had previously been off limits. Kids love this activity!

Remind adults to feel free to come up with their babies and help manipulate their babies' hands to pull Humpty off of the wall, if needed. For nonwalkers who are in their parents' arms, place Humpty's wall at the top of the flannel board and have the top of Humpty sticking out above the top of the easel. Even the youngest child should be able to use the grasping reflex to pull Humpy off of his wall.

Recap

Interactive Rhymes/Rimas interactivas helps foster several positive traits and skills:

- Performing an easily achievable task that is recognized and applauded by all builds a child's self-esteem.
- Learning how to take turns and to appreciate the achievements of others enhances social development.
- Children learn self-regulation by coming up to the flannel board when they are ready and going back to their place when their turn is over.

10. Closing Section/Despedida

Always end with the same closing activities. The two Barbara Cass-Beggs' songs "Can You Kick with Two Feet?"/"¿Puedes patear con dos pies?" (during which everyone sits in place and has a chance to exercise various parts of their bodies) and "We're So Happy That Everyone Is Here"/"Estamos contentos" signify the end of the program on a positive note and encourage people to come back again next week. This closing section lets everyone know for sure that the program is over, but it also reminds them that that their presence at the program was appreciated. Another phrase, a sing-song "¡Adios a todos!"/"Good-bye everybody, see you next week!" reminds program participants that the program is ongoing, and we hope they will come back again. By always starting and ending the program in the same way, babies will learn quickly to recognize the ritual, which adds to their sense of security.

Recap

Closing Section/Despedida is the same every week:

- The same closing songs help children transition to the end.
- The program ends on a positive note.
- Everyone is reminded to come back next time.

Once the program is finished, you may want to take out developmentally appropriate toys for the children to play with and ask adults to fill out surveys. You can also use this time to give tours of the library or to sign people up for Summer Reading Clubs. The free play can last anywhere from 10 to 30 minutes and might then be followed by refreshments.

Notes

1. Eric Hill has written a number of books about the dog Spot.
2. Lucy Cousins has written a number of books about the mouse Maisy.

Chapter 8

A Script for One Program

The script in this chapter contains the words to all of the rhymes, songs, and fingerplays in one sample program. Included in this script are directions from the librarian to the parents and some developmental tips. *Although in your real program, you should only be using one language per activity*, both languages are included here to let you know what is being said in case you are not a Spanish speaker. Not all of the rhymes are direct translations from the other language. Poetic license was taken in some instances to ensure that the flavor, the rhythm, and the flow of the rhymes remained the same. Depending on your audience, feel free to mix and match—for instance, you might want to offer the majority of the program in Spanish but to present the animal song section only in English. Although in a real setting you should include a maximum of only two developmental tips per program, I have included more here just to illustrate what the tips might be and how they can be used with different rhymes.

Sample Program Script

1. Welcoming Comments ☺#3

Introduce yourself:
Welcome to the _____ library. Hi. My name is _____, and I am your librarian.

Explain how it works:
I will say everything twice. The first time you can listen; the second time, repeat it with me. If you already know the song or rhyme, please recite it with me both times.

Create a comfortable atmosphere:
Children this age don't sit perfectly still. It is fine if they want to get up and wander around.

1. Bienvenidos ☺#3

Quiero presentarme:
Buenos días, mi nombre es _____ y soy su bibliotecaria.

Explica como funciona el programa:
Voy a repetir todo dos veces. Escuche la primera vez, y la segunda vez, repita conmigo. Si ya sabe la canción o la rima, dígala las dos veces conmigo.

Produce un ambiente cómodo:
Los niños de esta edad no se sientan inmóviles. Es normal si quieran levantarse y caminar.

Set limits:
However, I'd like you to pretend there is an invisible semicircle in front of my flannel board, and if your child comes within this semicircle, I would like you to physically come up and get him and bring him back to his seat in the circle with you.

Set limits:
Please turn off your cell phones, and save all conversations until after the program has finished.

Explain:
Young children watch their parents very carefully and mimic what they are doing. If you want your child to get the most out of this program, it is very important for you to participate fully by singing all of the songs and doing all of the fingerplays with gusto and enthusiasm.

And now, on to the program.

2. Opening Rhymes and Reads ☺#4

"We're So Happy That Everyone Is Here"*

(Tap hands on knees while singing)

I'm so happy (2×)
That everyone is here.
We're so happy (3×)
That everyone is here.

"Old Mother Goose"

(Place Mother Goose piece on the flannel board)
Old Mother Goose
(Tap hands on legs)
When she wanted to wander
Would fly through the air
(Lift baby or move hands in arc over your head)

Establece límites:
Me gustaría que pensaran que hay un círculo invisible frente a mi tablera de franela. Si su niño entra en este círculo, por favor venga a buscarlo y siéntelo con usted.

Establece límites:
Por favor, apague sus teléfonos celulares y guarde todas las conversaciones hasta después del programa.

Explica:
Los niños miran a sus padres muy atentos e imitan lo que hacen. Si quiere que su niño logre el máximo de este programa, es muy importante que usted participe completamente, cantando todas las canciones y haciendo todos los juegos de dedos con entusiasmo y pasión.

Y ahora comencemos con el programa.

2. Rimas y lectura ☺#4

"Estamos contentos"

(Dese golpecitos en las rodillas mientras que cante)
Estoy contentos (2×)
Que todos están aquí.
Estamos contentos (3×)
Que todos están aquí.

"La vieja Mamá Gansa"

(Ponga a la vieja Mamá Gansa en la tablera de franela)
La vieja Mamá Gansa
(Dese golpecitos en las piernas)
Cuando quería pasear
Volaba por el aire
(Cargue a su bebé o mueva sus manos en forma de arco arriba de su cabeza)

On a very fine gander.
(Looking at the sea, sway from side to side)

Let's repeat this rhyme. If you have a baby, lift him up in an arc when I lift my hands in the air.
(Repeat the rhyme; then remove the piece from the flannel board and drop it into the storage bin)

(Place turtle illustration on the flannel board)

Now let's make one hand into a turtle, pulling his head in and out of the shell.

Here is my puppet friend, Tomasa the turtle. She would like to show you her dance to this song, "La tortuga Tomasa," giving each child a welcome kiss.

(Walk around the circle giving a kiss to each child and saying a greeting such as "¡Hola!" or "Buenos días!" while singing the following song or while playing track #6 from Trepsi, Volume 4, "La tortuga Tomasa")

"Good Morning, Mrs. Tomasa"

Good morning, Mrs. Tomasa,
Mrs. Tomasa, Mrs. Tomasa.
Good morning, Mrs. Tomasa,
Where are you?
I'm going for a walk,
A walk, a walk.
I'm going for a walk, a walk,
And saying, "Hello."

"Little Chicks Are Singing"

(Show book illustration from ¡Pío peep!, pp. 56–57, or from The Baby Chicks Sing by Nancy Abraham Hall and Jill Syverson-Stork, pp. 4–5)

The little chicks are singing "pío pío pío"
(Open and close hands)
When they're feeling hungry
(Rub tummy)

Mirando el mar.
(Mirando el mar, muévase de lado a lado)

Repitamos esta rima. Si tiene un bebé, levántelo en un arco cuando levanto mis manos.
(Repita la rima; entonces quite la gansa de la tablera de franela y guárdala)

(Ponga la ilustración de la tortuga en la tablera de franela)
Ahora hagamos con la mano como una tortuga, sacando y metiendo la cabeza en el caparazón.

Aquí está mi muñeca amiga, Tomasa. Ella quiere mostrarles su baile y después le dará un beso de saludo a cada niño.

(Camine alrededor del círculo dándole un beso a cada niño y diciéndole "¡Hola!" o "¡Buenos días!" en lo que cantan la canción siguiente o en lo que tocan la canción numero 6 de Trepsi, Volumen número 4, "La tortuga Tomasa")

"Buenos días, Señora Tomasa"

Buenos días, Señora Tomasa,
Señora Tomasa, Señora Tomasa.
Buenos días, Señora Tomasa,
¿Donde están usted?
Estoy tomando un paseo,
Un paseo, un paseo.
Estoy tomando un paseo, un paseo,
Y saludando, "Hola."

"Los pollitos dicen"

(Enseñe la ilustración del libro ¡Pio peep!, pp. 56–57 o de Los pollitos dicen escrito por Nancy Abraham Hall y Jill Syverson-Stork, pp. 4–5)

Los pollitos dicen pío pío pío
(Abra y cierre las manos)
Cuando tienen hambre
(Frótese la barriga)

When they're feeling cold.
(Hug yourself and shiver)
Mother hen is looking for some corn and wheat.
(Make pecking motions with hands)

She gives her children food.
(Touch mouth)
She keeps her children warm.
(Hug yourself)
The little chicks are cuddled underneath her wings.
(Extend bent arm in front of you and slightly rock)
The little chicks are sleeping
(Close eyes, lean head to side on hands)

Until the morning comes.

Wake up!
(Open eyes, sit up straight)

(Hold up a copy of the book Where's Spot? *by Eric Hill)*

This is *Where's Spot?* by Eric Hill. Please help me out by saying what is under each flap.

(Read the book Where's Spot? *from cover to cover)*

And that is *Where's Spot?* by Eric Hill.
(Drop book in storage bin)

Developmental tip: *(After reading one, very short book cover to cover)* A great way to promote reading is to read books aloud to your child.

Cuando tienen frío.
(Abrácese y tiembla)
La gallina busca el maíz y el trigo.

(Haga gestos con las manos que parezcan picotazos)
Les da la comida.
(Tóquese la boca)
Les presta abrigo.
(Abrácese)
Bajo sus alas, acurrucaditos.

(Estire los brazos como si estuviera meciendo a un bebe)
Duermen los pollitos
(Cierre los ojos y acueste la cabeza para el lado sobre las manos)
Hasta el otro día.

¡Despiértense!
(Abra los ojos, siéntese derecho)

(Enseñe el libro ¿Donde está Spot? *escrito por Eric Hill)*

Este es *¿Donde está Spot?* escrito por Eric Hill. Por favor ayúdame diciendo lo que está debajo de cada faldilla.

(Lea el libro ¿Donde está Spot? *entero)*

Y ese es *¿Donde está Spot?* escrito por Eric Hill. *(Guarde el libro)*

Consejo de desarrollo: *(Ésto es después de leer)* Una buena manera de promover la lectura es leer libros en voz alta con su hijo.

"We Hit the Floor Together"*

We hit the floor together,
We hit the floor together,
We hit the floor together,
Because it's fun to do.

We wiggle our fingers together, (3×)
Because it's fun to do.

"Pegamos el piso juntos"

Pegamos el piso juntos,
Pegamos el piso juntos,
Pegamos el piso juntos,
Porque es divertido.

Movemos los dedos juntos, (3×)
Porque es divertido.

We all wave hello, (3×)
Because it's fun to do.

3. Body Rhymes ☻#5

HEAD

Follow along with us, but do the movement on your child's head.

"Where Is My Head?"

Where is my head?
Knock, knock, here it is.
Where are my ears?
Tickle, tickle, here they are.
Where is my nose?
Here it is!

FINGERS

"Fingers Like to Wiggle Waggle"*

(Begin each verse by wiggling fingers of both hands in front of you)

Fingers like to wiggle waggle,
Wiggle waggle, wiggle waggle.
Fingers like to wiggle waggle
Way up high!

(Continue wiggling fingers while reaching straight up; say "high" in a very high voice)

Fingers like to wiggle waggle,
Wiggle waggle, wiggle waggle.
Fingers like to wiggle waggle
Way down low!

(Continue wiggling fingers while lowering hands; say "low" in a very low voice)

Fingers like to wiggle waggle,
Wiggle waggle, wiggle waggle.
Fingers like to wiggle waggle
On my knees!

(Place fingers on knees)

Saludamos hola, (3×)
Porque es divertido.

3. Rimas del cuerpo ☻#5

CABEZA

Siga con nosotros pero haga los movimientos en la cabeza de su niño.

"¿Dónde está mi cabeza?"

¿Dónde está mi cabeza?
Ton, ton, aquí está.
¿Dónde están mis orejas?
Hacen cosquillas, cosquillas.
¿Dónde está mi naríz?
¡Aquí, tócala asi!

LOS DEDITOS

"A los deditos les gusta moverse"*

(Empiece cada verso moviendo sus dedos delante de usted)

A los deditos les gusta moverse,
Asi asá, asi asá.
A los deditos les gusta moverse
¡Hacía arriba!

(Siga moviendo sus dedos en lo que estira sus brazos para arriba; diga "arriba" en voz alta)

A los deditos les gusta moverse,
Asi asá, asi asá.
A los deditos les gusta moverse
¡Hacía abajo!

(Continúe moviendo los dedos y baje las manos; diga "abajo" en una voz bien baja)

A los deditos les gusta moverse,
Asi asá, asi asá.
A los deditos les gusta moverse
¡Sobre las rodillas!

(Ponga sus dedos en sus rodillas)

(NOTE: In place of the Spanish translation for "Fingers Like to Wiggle, Waggle," which is song #19 in Chapter 13, you may want to use the traditional Spanish rhyme "Tengo manitas." This traditional hand rhyme is used on the CD, in place of the Spanish translation for "Fingers Like to Wiggle Waggle.")

HANDS

"Here Are My Hands"

Here are my hands.
(Show open hands)
Where are my hands?
(Put hands behind back)
Let's take a peek.
(One hand over eyes, peering)
They're playing hide-and-seek!
(Show open hands again)

(Because "Tengo manitas" was used in place of the Spanish translation for "Fingers Like to Wiggle Waggle," this English translation is not included on the accompanying CD.)

"Little Tortillas for Mother/ Potatoes and Potatoes"

(Show the cover illustration from Tortillitas para mamá *by Margot C. Griego et al.; slap hands together as if making tortillas)*

Little tortillas for mama.
Little tortillas for papa.
The warm ones for mama.
The nice ones for papa.
Potatoes, potatoes for papa.
Potatoes, potatoes for mama.
The nice ones are for papa.
The warm ones are for mama.

(NOTE: This translation is not included on the accompanying CD.)

(En vez de usar la traducción de "A los deditosos les gusta moverse," quizás quiera usar la rima tradicional en español, "Tengo manitas" que sigue o "Cinco deditos.")

MANITAS

"Tengo manitas"

Tengo manitas.
(Abra las manos)
No tengo manitas.
(Esconda las manos atrás de su espalda)
Porque las tengo.
(Abra las manos)
Desconchabadita.
(Esconda las manos atrás de su espalda)

(Because this rhyme was used to show how substitutions can be done, it can be found immediately following the Spanish translation of "Fingers Like to Wiggle Waggle" on the CD. This is an example of a traditional Spanish rhyme being used in place of a translated English one.)

"Tortillitas para mamá/Papas y papas"

(Enseñe la portada del libro Tortillitas para mamá *escrito por Margo C. Griego et al.; pegue las manos como si estuviera haciendo tortillitas)*

Tortillitas para mamá.
Tortillitas para papá.
Las doraditas para mamá.
Las bonitas para papá.
Papas y papas para papá.
Papas y papas para mamá
Las bonitas para papá.
Las calientitas para mamá.

"Eency Weency Spider/Great Big Spider"

(With spider puppets)

The eency weency spider
Crawled up the water spout.
Down came the rain
And washed the spider out.
Out came the sun
And dried up all the rain.
And the eency weency spider
Went up the spout again.

(Spider puppet says) Everyone always sings about my brother, la araña pequeñita. But no one sings about me, la araña grandotota. I am so sad, I am going to cry.

(Puppet pretends to cry)

Would you like us to sing about you?

(Spider) Yes, please.

Okay. Everyone, take out your great big hands, your great big voices, and make great big movements for "La araña grandotota."

(Sing in a deep voice with exaggerated movements)

The great big spider
Crawled up the water spout.
Down came the rain
And washed the spider out.
Out came the sun
And dried up all the rain.
And the great big spider
Went up the spout again.

(Spider puppet to presenter) That was so great, I am going to give you a great big kiss. . . .

(If there is a small group, walk around the circle and give spider kisses to each child)

"La araña pequeñita/La araña grandotota"

(Con títeres de arañas)

La araña pequeñita
Subió subió subió.
Vino la lluvia
Y se la llevó.
Salió el sol
Y todo lo secó.
La araña pequeñita
Subió subió subió.

(El títere araña dice) Todo el mundo siempre canta de mi hermano, la araña pequeñita. Pero nadie cante de mí, la araña grandotota. Estoy tan triste que voy a llorar.
(El títere se hace el que está llorando)

¿Quiere que cantemos de ti?

(La araña) Sí, por favor.

Bueno, todos, sacan las manos grandotas, sus voces profundas profundas, y hagan movimientos grandotes para "La araña grandotota."

(Cante en una voz profunda con movimientos exagerados)

La araña grandotota
Subió subió subió.
Vino la lluvia
Y se la llevó.
Salió el sol
Y todo lo secó.
La araña grandotota
Subió subió subió.

(La marioneta araña a la presentadora) Eso estuvo magnífico que voy a darte un beso grandotoe. . . .

(Si hay un grupo pequeño, camine alrededor del circulo y dele besos de araña a cada niño)

KNEES

Now, please put your feet out straight on the floor in front of you, and put your child on your knees facing me. Start bouncing your knees up and down for some fun knee-bouncing rhymes.

"This Is the Way the Ladies Ride"

(Say each phrase faster than the one before)

This is the way the ladies ride . . .
Lim, lim, lim
This is way the gentlemen ride . . .
Trim, trim, trim
This is the way the farmers ride . . .
Trot, trot, trot
Sometimes they jump the fence.
And sometimes they fall to the ground!

"Giddy-Up My Horse"

Giddy-up my horse, hey! (3×)
Jump up high!
Giddy-up my horse, hey! (3×)
Don't fall down!
Giddy-up my horse, hey! (3×)
Here we go over!

(Instead of using the rhymes above, there are many other wonderful ones. "The Grand Old Duke of York" in English is one, and a traditional Spanish rhyme that lends itself well to knee bounces could be another.)

"Jack and Jill"

(Show illustration for this poem from The Little Dog Laughed *by Lucy Cousins)*

Jack and Jill went up the hill
(Bounce child on lap)
To fetch a pail of water.
Jack fell down,
(Lean to one side)
And rolled around,
(Lean to the other side)

RODILLAS

Ahora estirenlas piernas en el piso y ponga a su hijo en sus rodillas mirando hacia mí. Comience a rebotar para arriba y abajo y siga las rimas divertidas.

"Así al caballo montan las damas"

(Diga cada frase un poquito mas rápido)

Así al caballo montan las damas,
Ta ta ta
Así cabalgan los caballeros,
Ta ta ta
Así montan los campesinos,
Ta ta ta
A veces saltan la barrera.
A veces chocan con la tierra.

"Ándale caballo"

¡Ándale caballo, (3×)
¡Hacia arriba!
¡Ándale caballo, (3×)
¡Hacia abajo!
¡Ándale caballo, (3×)
¡Hacia al lado!

(En vez de usar la rima que arriba aparece, hay otras maravillosas opciones. "El gran Duque de York" en inglés es una opción, y/o una rima tradicional en español que permita brincar al bebé sobre las rodillas.)

"Juan y Juana"

(Enseñe la ilustración de este poema usando El perrito se rió *escrito por Lucy Cousins)*

Juan y Juana subieron al monte
(Brinque el bebe en el regazo)
En busca de un cubo de agua.
Juan se cayó,
(Inclínese para un lado)
La crisma se rompió,
(Inclínese para el otro lado)

And Jill went tumbling after.
(Bounce very quickly)

4. Rum Pum Pum Drum Sequence ☉#6

"Rum Pum Pum"*

(Children tap out names with syllables)

Rum pum pum. This is my drum.
Rum pum pum. This is my drum.
My name is ___. What's your name?

(Presenter) Now say your child's name and help him hit the drum.

(Presenter walks around giving each child a chance to tap their name on the drum according to the syllables; when they do, say a greeting like "¡Hola!" or "Buenos días")

(Presenter) Everyone, stand up!

5. Standing-Up Activities ☉#7

"And We Walk"

And we walk, and we walk, and we walk,
and we stop. (3×)
And we all turn around! WHOOOO!

And we run, and we run, and we run,
and we stop. (3×)
And we all turn around! WHOOOO!

(Shake the tambourine vigorously while everyone turns around)

And we jump, and we jump, and we jump,
and we stop. (3×)
And we all turn around! WHOOOO!

(Substitute "walk" with other words and motions, such as "run," "creep," "tiptoe," "jump," or "march")

Y Juana se despeñó en la zanja.
(Brinque rápidamente)

4. Sequencia de "rum pum peta" ☉#6

"Rum pum peta"

(Los niños dan golpecitos para cada sílaba de su nombre)

Rum pum peta. Escucha mi pandereta.
Rum pum peta. Escucha mi pandereta.
Mi nombre es ___. ¿Y tu?

(Presentador) Ahora diga el nombre de su hijo y ayúdelo a tocar la pandereta.

(El presentador le da una oportunidad a cada niño para que pueda tocar la pandereta con una palmadita para cada sílaba de su nombre; cuando lo haga, diga "¡Hola!" o "Buenos días")

(Presentador) ¡Parénse, todos!

5. Actividades al pararse ☉#7

"Y caminamos"

Y caminamos, caminamos, caminamos,
y paramos. (3×)
¡Y demos una vuelta! ¡JUUUUU!

Y corremos, y corremos, y corremos,
y paramos. (3×)
¡Y demos una vuelta! ¡JUUUUU!

(Mueva el tamborín mucho en lo que todo el mundo da una vuelta)

Y brincamos, y brincamos, y brincamos,
y paramos. (3×)
¡Y demos una vuelta! ¡JUUUUU!

(Substituya "camina" con otras palabras y movimientos: "corremos," "arrastramos," "vayamos de puntillas," "brinquemos," o "marchemos")

"The Chirimbolo Game"

The chirimbolo game
How much fun it is!
One foot, the other foot
One hand, the other hand
One elbow, the other elbow.
The nose and the mouth.

"Stir It, Stir the Chocolate"

Stir it, stir it, stir the chocolate.
You have a peanut nose.
One, two, three, CHO!
One, two, three, CO!
One, two, three, LA!
One, two, three, TE!
Chocolate, chocolate!
Stir it, stir it, stir the chocolate!
(Lower voice and body)
Stir it, stir it, stir it, stir it,
Stir it, stir it, stir the CHOCOLATE!
(Jump up and shout)

Now we eat the chocolate and sit down.

6. Animals! ☻#8

(Show book illustrations of farm animals from Eric Carle's The Very Busy Spider, *while singing this song to match the illustrations)*

"I Went to Visit the Farm"

I went to visit a farm one day.
I saw a horse along the way.
And what do you think the horse did say?
["Neigh, neigh."]

(Substitute with: "cow," "sheep," "pig," "dog," "duck," "rooster")

"El juego chirimbolo"

El juego chirimbolo
¡Qué bonito es!
Un pie, otro pie,
Una mano, otra mano
Un codo, otro codo.
La nariz y la boca.

"Bate, bate, chocolate"

Bate, bate, chocolate.
Tu nariz de cacahuate.
Uno, dos, tres, ¡CHO!
Uno, dos, tres, ¡CO!
Uno, dos, tres, ¡LA!
Uno, dos, tres, ¡TE!
Chocolate, ¡chocolate!
Bate, bate, ¡chocolate!
(Baje la voz y el cuerpo)
Bate, bate, bate, bate,
Bate, bate, ¡CHOCOLATE!
(Brinque y grite)

Y ahora comemos el chocolate y nos sentamos.

6.¡Animales! ☻#8

(Enseñe las ilustraciones del los animales de finca del libro de Eric Carle La araña muy ocupada, *en lo que canta esta canción)*

"Fui a visitar la granja"

Fui a visitar la granja un día.
Por allí vi un caballo.
¿Qué crees que dijo el caballo?
["Jeeee, jeeee."]

(Substituye con: "vaca," "oveja," "cerdo," "perro," "pato," "gallo")

"When the [Cats] Get Up in the Morning"

(Pull puppets out of a duffel bag one by one while singing the verse about that animal)

When the [cats] get up in the morning,
they always say "[Meow]!"
When the [cats] get up in the morning,
they say, "[Meow, Meow]!"

(Substitute with: "dogs," "cows," "horses," "pigs," "roosters," "hens," "ducks," "geese")

"One Elephant Went Out to Play"

(Place elephant puppet on outstretched legs or show illustration from The Baby Chicks Sing *by Nancy Abraham Hall and Jill Syverson-Stork, pp. 10–11)*

One elephant went out to play
Upon a spider's web one day.
He had such enormous fun
That he called for another elephant to come.

Two elephants went out to play
Upon a spider's web one day.
They had such enormous fun
That they called for another elephant to come.

"Hickory Dickory Dare"

Hey, look over there!
The pig flew up in the air!
(Throw a stuffed animal pig into the air)
Farmer Brown soon brought her down,
Hickory, dickory dare!

Now each child is going to have a turn to throw the pig up in the air. When they do, let's give them a big round of applause for a job well done.

"Cuando los [gatos] se despiertan"

(Saque los peluches, uno por uno, de una bolsa mientras canta el verso del animal que corresponde)

Cuando los [gatos] se despiertan,
siempre dicen "¡[Miau]!"
Cuando los [gatos] se despiertan,
siempre dicen "¡[Miau, miau]!"

(Substitutye con: "los perros," "las vacas," "los caballos," "los cerdos," "los gallos," "las gallinas," "los patos," "los gansos")

"Un elefante se balanceaba"

(Ponga el títere del elefante en sus piernas o enseñe la ilustración de Los Pollitos Dicen *escrito por Nancy Abraham Hall y Jill Syverson-Stork, pp. 10–11)*

Un elefante se balanceaba
Sobre la tela de una araña.
Como veía que resistía
Fue a llamar a otro elefante.

Dos elefantes se balanceaban
Sobre la tela de una araña.
Como veían que resistía
Fueron a llamar a otro elefante.

"El cochinito"

¡Mire el cochinito!
¡Voló por el aire!
(Tire el cerdo de peluche al aire)
Muy pronto lo bajó,
¡Ay! hacer un baile.

Ahora cada niño va a tener una oportunidad de tirar el cerdo en el aire. Cuando lo hacen, vamos a aplaudirle por hacerlo bien.

(Walk around the semicircle, handing the pig to each child. Say "1, 2, 3" and clap when they release the pig. If the child has difficulty letting go, gently take hold of the pig part facing you, and slowly move hands up and down with the child to the rhythm of the "1, 2, 3." Tug a little harder on "3" and the child will release the animal.)

(Camine alrededor del semicírculo, dándole el cerdo a cada niño. Diga "1, 2, 3" y aplaude cuando suelta el cerdo. Si el niño tiene dificultad soltando el puerco, suavemente mueva sus manos para arriba y abajo con el niño en lo que digan "1, 2, 3." Hale el puerco más fuerte en "3" y el niño soltará el animal.)

7. Musical Instruments and Props

7. Instrumentos musicales y accesorios

BELLS ☻#9

(Walk around the inside of the semicircle, handing one bell from your canvas bag to each child and each adult)

CAMPANILLAS ☻#9

(Camine en el centro del semicírculo, dándole una campana a cada niño de su bolsa)

"We Ring Our Bells Together"*

We ring our bells together,
We ring our bells together,
We ring our bells together,
Because it's fun to do. (2×)

Ring them up HIGH.
Ring them down LOW.
Ring them in the MIDDLE.

"Toquemos campanillas"

Toquemos campanillas,
Toquemos campanillas,
Toquemos campanillas,
Porque es divertido. (2×)

Tócalas ARRIBA.
Tócalas ABAJO.
Tócalas en el MEDIO.

"Are You Sleeping, Brother John?"

(Sung to the tune of "Frère Jacques")

Are you sleeping? Are you sleeping?
Brother John, Brother John
Morning bells are ringing. (2×)
Ding dang dong. (2×)

(Play a short piece of recorded music and ask everyone to ring their bells in time to the music)

Here is a traditional Spanish rhyme called "Teresa, la Marquesa":

"Martinillo"

(Frère Jacques)

Martinillo, martinillo
¿Dónde estás? ¿Dónde estás?
Toca la campana. (2×)
Din don dan. (2×)

(Toque una canción y dígale a todo el mundo que toquen sus campanas con la música)

Aquí está la tradicional que se llama "Teresa, la marquesa":

"Teresa, the Queen"

Teresa, the queen,
Tippiti tippiti teen.
Upon her head a crown,
(Put your hands above your head in the shape of a crown)
Tippiti tippiti town.

She rings four bells,
Tippiti tippiti tells.
She tip toes here and there,
Tippiti tippiti tear.

"Bells Away"*

(While singing this, walk around the semicircle with an open canvas bags. Children and adults will drop bells into the bag. Remind them to put any wet bells into your hand.)

Bells away, bells away
Put the bells away today.

SCARVES ☮ #10

"Wind, Oh Wind"*

Wind, oh wind, oh wind, I say,
What are you blowing away today?
Scarves, oh scarves, oh scarves, I say.
The wind is blowing the scarves away.

Game: Peek-a-Boo, I See You*

Peek-a-boo, I see you! I see you smiling there. (2×)

(Walk around circle playing scarf peek-a-boo with each child)

(Presenter) Scrunch up your scarves and pretend they are washcloths.

"Teresa, la marquesa"

Teresa, la marquesa,
Tipiti, tipitesa.
Tenia una corona,
(Ponga sus manos arriba de su cabeza como si fuera una corona)
Tipiti, tiritona.

Con cuatro campanillas,
Tipiti, tipitillas
Y caminaba de puntillas,
Tipiti, tipiton.

"Entréguenlas campanas"

(En lo que canta esto, camine alrededor del semicírculo con una bolsa abierta. Los niños y adultos guardaran sus campanas en la bolsa. Digales que pongan las campanas mojadas en su mano.)

Entréguenlas, entréguenlas
Pongamos todo en su lugar.

PAÑUELOS ☮ #10

"Viento, ay viento"

Viento, viento, viento siento,
¿Qué vas a llevar hoy?
Pañuelo, pañuelo, pañuelo, al suelo.
El viento lleva el pañuelo al suelo.

"Peek-a-boo"

Peek-a-boo, ¿Quién está, quién está, alli? (2×)

(Ande alrededor y juegue peek-a-boo con cada niño)

(Presentador) Arruguen sus bufandas y imaginen que son toallitas.

"This Is the Way We Wash"

This is the way we wash our face, wash our
face, wash our face
This is the way we wash our face,
So early in the morning.

(Substitute with: "neck," "arms," "knees")

"Scarves Away"*

[Scarves] away, [scarves] away
Put the [scarves] away today.

(Walk around the circle, collecting the scarves)

Developmental tip: *(After collecting all of the
musical instruments, sing "Entréguenlas" and
add this developmental tip)* Singing a clean-
up song makes cleaning up a fun activity
for children and teaches them what behavior you expect when it is time to put something away. Cleaning up with a song is
gentle and loving and seems much more
like fun than a chore.

8. "Lullabies" ⊙#11

Now put your children on your lap, hold
them closely so they can hear your heartbeat, and rock back and forth while singing
this lullaby.

"Twinkle, Twinkle, Little Star"

(Sing slowly)
Twinkle, twinkle, little star
How I wonder where you are.
Up above the world so high
Like a diamond in the sky.
Twinkle, twinkle, little star
How I wonder where you are.

"Así vamos a lavarnos"

Así vamos a lavarnos la cara, lavarnos la
cara, lavarnos la cara,
Así vamos a lavarnos la cara
Con el pañuela.

(Substituye con: "cuello," "brazos," "rodillas")

"Entréguenlos, entréguenlos"

Entréguenlos, entréguenlos
Pongamos todo en su lugar.

*(Camine alrededor del circulo, coleccione las
bufandas)*

Consejo de desarrollo: *(Ésto sigue después de
que los niños entreguen los instrumentos musicales y canten "Entréguenlos")* Cantando una
canción de la limpieza hace que el limpiar
sea una actividad divertida para los niños y
los enseña comportarse cuando necesitan
poner algo en su sitio. Limpiando con una
canción es dócil y cariñoso y más como un
juego que un trabajo de la casa.

8. "Cancioncitas" ⊙#11

Ahora ponga su niño en su regazo, abrácelo
cerca para que oiga los latidos de su
corazón, y cante este cancioncita mientras
lo acunas para adelante y para atrás.

"Estrellita dónde estás"

(Cante despacio)
Estrellita dónde estás
Me pregunto que serás.
En el cielo, en el mar
Un diamante de verdad.
Estrellita, dónde estás
Me pregunto qué serás.

9. Interactive Rhymes ☉#12

"Jack Be Nimble"

Jack, be nimble!
Jack, be quick!
Jack, jump over
The candlestick.

(Presenter places candlestick on the floor and stands in front of it; she jumps over the candlestick, turns around, and jumps back over)

Now I'd like to invite each child to have a turn coming up and jumping over the candlestick. Let's give a big round of applause each time they do this to celebrate their accomplishment. Then they can return to the circle so another child can have a turn.

(If your group consists of very young babies, you may want to alter the activity, walking around the inside of the semicircle and placing the candlestick in front of each parent with a baby on their lap; the parents can then lift their children over the candlestick)

(When finished, place the candlestick in the storage bin and take out the flannel pieces for Humpty Dumpty and his wall)

"Humpty Dumpty"

(Give instructions for using flannel characters)

Humpty Dumpty sat on a wall.
Humpty Dumpty had a great fall.
(Sweep Humpy off of the wall with a large hand movement)
All the king's horses and all the king's men
Couldn't put Humpty together again.

(Take Humpty off the floor and put him back on the wall)

(Presenter) Now I'd like each child to come up and have a turn pulling Humpty off of his wall. When they do, let's give each child a big round of applause for a job well done.

9. Rimas interactivas ☉#12

"¡Juan alerta!"

¡Juan, alerta!
¡Juan, ligero!
Salta la vela
Y el candelero.

(Póngale el candelero en el piso y párese en frente de él y brinque sobre el candelero; dé una vuelta y brinque otra vez sobre el candelero para devolver donde comenzó)

Ahora quisiera invitar a cada niño que tenga su turno de brincar el candelero. Vamos a aplaudir cada vez que lo hace para celebrar su éxito. Después que lo hace, puede regresar al círculo para que otro niño tenga su turno.

(Si los niños en su grupo son bebes, pueden poner el candelero delante de cada padre y dejar que ellos carguen/brinquen a su bebe sobre el candelero)

(Cuando terminen, guarde el candelero y saque los pedazos de franela para Jamti Damti)

"Jamti Damti"

(Explique cómo usar los muñecos de franela)

Jamti Damti se sentó en un muro.
Jamti Damti se cayó muy duro.
(Quite a Jamti de la pared con un movimiento grande)
Ni la guardia civil ni la caballería
Sabían cómo se incorporaría.

(Recoja a Jamti del piso y póngalo en la pared de nuevo)

(Presentador) Ahora quisiera que cada niño venga y tome un turno tumbándo a Jamti de la pared. Y cuando lo hagan, aplaudiremos a cada niño para animarlo.

Everyone gets just one turn, so when each child's turn is done, if they don't go back to their seat on their own, parents should come up and bring them back to their seats. This is a great exercise for teaching turn-taking and patience.

(When all children have had a turn, recite the rhyme again, pulling Humpty off of his wall)

A cada niño le toca un turno. Cuando se acaba su turno si no vuelve a sentarse, padres, por favor, ayúdelo a sentarse.

(Cuando todos los niños hayan tenido una oportunidad de tumbar a Jamti, repita la rima otra vez y quite a Jamti de la pared)

10. Closing Section ☺#13

"Can You Kick with Two Feet?"*

Can you kick with two feet,
two feet, two feet?
Can you kick with two feet,
kick kick kick kick kick.
Can you kiss with two lips,
two lips, two lips?
Can you kiss with two lips,
mua mua mua mua mua.
Can you wave bye-bye, bye-bye, bye-bye?
Can you wave bye-bye, bye-bye bye-bye bye.

"We're So Happy"*

We're so happy, We're so happy,
We're so happy that everyone is here. (2×)

Bye everybody! See you next time!

10. Despedida ☺#13

"¿Puedes patear con dos pies?"

¿Puedes patear con dos pies,
dos pies, dos pies?
Puedes patear con dos pies,
pa pa pa pa pa.
¿Puedes besar con dos labios,
dos labios, dos labios?
Puedes besar con dos labios,
mua mua mua mua mua.
¿Puedes decir adiós, adiós, adiós?
Puedes decir adiós, adiós, adiós.

"Estamos contentos"

Estamos contentos, estamos contentos,
estamos contentos que todos están aquí. (2×)

¡Adios a todos!

Notes: Special thanks to Anne Calderón, Rosa Hernandez, Gilda Martinez, Gilda Valdes, Jennifer Bown-Olmedo, Iris Cotto, Melissa Da, and Evelio Méndez for their help with the Spanish. Information about each rhyme, including authorship, adaptor, lyrics, and translation credits, can be found in Chapter 13.

*All starred rhymes were either written or adapted by Barbara Cass-Beggs (1904–1990), the music educator from Canada who believed in the development of the whole child by facilitating cheerful interactions with the caregiving adults through structured playful, musical interactions. Her songs use easy vocabulary words and are simple to sing; taken as part of the entire program, they further Barbara's goal of helping each child gain confidence and security. Barbara's Listen, Like, Learn approach uses principles established by Kodály and Orff. Barbara based her musical programs for parents and babies upon research suggesting that singing assists in a baby's development. Similar to her Your Baby Needs Music program, Mother Goose on the Loose en Español strengthens bonding between parent and child, develops speech by building neural pathways in the brain, incorporates lullabies that are soothing for both adult and child, and is simply great fun.

Resources Used

Books

Ada, Alma Flor. 2003. *!Pio Peep! Traditional Spanish Nursery Rhymes* (Bilingual). New York: HarperCollins.

Carle, Eric. 1995. *The Very Busy Spider.* New York: Penguin.

Cousins, Lucy. 1990. *The Little Dog Laughed.* New York: Dutton.

Griego, Margot C., Betsy L. Bucks, Sharon S. Gilbert, and Laurel H. Kimball. 1988. *Tortillitas para mamá and Other Nursery Rhymes* (Bilingual Edition in Spanish and English). New York: Henry Holt.

Hall, Nancy Abraham, and Jill Syverson-Stork. 1994. *The Baby Chicks Sing/Los pollitos dicen.* New York: Little, Brown, pp. 10–11.

Hill, Eric. 1996. *¿Donde Esta Spot?/Where's Spot?* New York: Puffin.

Recordings

Trepsi, 2003, Volume 4, Track #6. "La tortuga Tomasa." *La tortuga Tomasa.* Centro de estimulación y desarrollo infantil. CD.

Chapter 9

Using Music in Your Program

There are many reasons to use music in your programs and many ways to do so.

Singing

Singing to babies can help focus their attention, comfort them, nurture them, and provide a means of communication. It exposes them to words and helps increase their vocabulary. The awareness of pitch has been connected with phonological awareness, which helps in learning how to read (Weinberger, 1998: 39). In addition to being fun, musical fingerplays are multisensory experiences that combine movement, music, and language, which "wire" brain connections. These connections help children's learning (Honig, 1995).

Singing also helps to develop vocabulary. While memorizing a poem may be a difficult task, learning those same words set to music may be much easier! Parents who do not speak English may be hesitant to sing to their children in Spanish, mistakenly thinking that it is better for their young children to learn only English in order not to confuse it with another language. This is a fallacy. Studies have shown that children who have rich vocabularies *in any language* will have an easier time in school, even if the language of instruction in the school they will attend is English and the songs they know are in another language (see Chapter 2 for more information). Reassuring parents that it is not only fine but beneficial for them to sing to their young children also serves a greater purpose by encouraging the child's development and strengthening the bond between parent and child.

By using Spanish-language songs in your library programs you are sending the message to parents that it is okay for them to sing to their children in Spanish, and by doing so you are establishing model behavior. If the librarian can sing in Spanish, surely it is fine for the parents to sing in Spanish too! You may be reawakening their memories of songs from their childhood that they may have forgotten, or you could be teaching them new songs in their own native language. Don't forget that there are many different dialects and versions of both spoken and written Spanish. Adult participants may tell you that you are singing the "wrong" version of a traditional song, or they may disagree among themselves as to what constitutes the "proper" version of this song. When this occurs, refer to the information about using the Spanish language discussed in the Introduction and in Chapter 1 of this book.

A comprehensive resource of Spanish-language songs for children can be found at "Mama Lisa's World en Español at www.mamalisa.com/?t=sh. A link to a bilingual Mother Goose on the Loose CD with both Spanish and English developmental tips can be found at www.mgol.org.

Including some songs in English helps non-English-speaking adults increase their own vocabularies. Singing the songs in English week after week gives them the experience of using English words and helps them develop confidence in articulating those words. Because of this, many educators shy away from using nonsense words or phrases such as "Hickory Dickory," believing it is important to stick to "real" words. Nonsense words in nursery rhymes, however, often have a lyrical sound and a lovely beat. Some of these rhymes are well-known throughout the English-speaking world and being familiar with them can be helpful. Being able to recite "Hickory Dickory Dock" and other classic rhymes along with their kindergarten teacher at the beginning of their first year in school will help children from non-English-speaking homes feel confident in their English-language abilities.

Don't worry if you do not have a beautiful singing voice or if you cannot stay on key! Keep in mind that your main goal is to facilitate interaction between the adults and their children and not to give a five star performance. In fact, if your voice is less than perfect, you may be positively modeling the fact that adults do not need terrific voices in order to sing to and with their children. If you are very insecure about your voice, you may want to create a CD of the songs you will be using and *sing along* with the CD whenever you use it in your program.

The Steady Beat

While still a fetus in mother's womb, music can influence (Cass-Beggs, 1991)! The sounds of mother's heartbeat, breathing, and circulation provide a steady beat while voices and music also filter in. Hearing these sounds forms the beginning of listening. Once the baby is born, hearing and moving to a steady beat can be very comforting. Scientific studies suggest that children who can keep a steady beat seem to have a better ability to read and more organized thought patterns. In addition to enjoying the sound of a steady beat, children can experience it directly through knee bounces, clapping and tapping games, rocking during lullabies, and marching to music. This is why many programs for babies often include these types of activities. Nursery rhymes are perfect for young children because they are set to simple melodies that are easy to hear and repeat, they generally have a steady beat, and they can include a wide variety of vocabulary words.

In addition to singing, simply listening to music and hearing songs also has a profound effect on young children. Research indicates that learning to listen to music can raise reading scores significantly (Weinberger, 1998). Children can learn from music and also develop an appreciation for it.

Listening

Listening is different from hearing. Hearing is simply absorbing the sounds around you—a passive activity—whereas listening means actively focusing on some sounds while filtering out others. Listening to what other people are saying is a valuable social skill, learning to focus and respond to specific sounds helps to develop one's attention span, and listening to different types of music can help children develop an appreciation for it. Listening to music can affect mood—soft music can calm, lively music can help people feel energetic, and other types of music may conjure up pictures in the mind.

The Listen, Like, Learn approach of Barbara Cass-Beggs asserts that listening to music helps children become familiar with it. Once they are familiar with it, they grow to like it. And, once they like it, it is easy to learn from it. If you are driving in a car and hear a song on the radio for the first time, you may want to switch the channel. The song may seem strange and you may not like it. If that same song is played repeatedly throughout the next few days, you may start to learn some of the lyrics without even trying. When the songs come on the radio again, you may find yourself suddenly singing along with it rather than changing the channel! This is a clear illustration of the Listen, Like, Learn approach.

Throughout the Spanish-speaking world, there are many different types of music, musical instruments, and dances, including flamenco, joto, trikitixa, salsa, and rumba. In the United States, popular varieties of music include classical, rock-and-roll, country, bluegrass, klezmer, gospel, and zydeco. Because people love hearing music that they are already familiar with and exposure to wide varieties of music can enhance musical appreciation and lead to greater learning opportunities, it is worthwhile to pay attention to the recorded music you play during your programs.

Using Musical Instruments and Props

By distributing percussion instruments and asking everyone to "play to the beat," the attraction of the steady beat will be combined with the encouragement and practice of listening skills. Simple percussion instruments especially appropriate for young children are shakers, bells, rhythm sticks, and simple drums.

The youngest children will not be able to manipulate the instruments by themselves but will enjoy watching and listening to their parent or caregiver. As their motor skills develop, the children will be able to start using the instruments to play a steady beat. In addition to instruments, colored scarves can also be used successfully with music. Children can wave, throw, or blow the scarves, play peek-a-boo, or pretend that they are other things such as washcloths or leaves falling from a tree. Scarves can be waved to recorded music to reflect the tone—quickly, slowly, furiously, gently, in swirls or in a straight pattern, etc. Using any or all of these props enhances the early educational experience. Try using a wide variety of music during the part of your program when musical instruments are distributed and everyone is asked to play along with the beat!

Resources

There are many good CDs with children's songs in Spanish that can be used in your program. José-Luis Orozco is a well-known musician who has wonderful compilations of traditional Spanish-language children's songs. Information on his books and songs can be found at www.joseluisorozco.com. Another group, Trepsi, has a number of CDs with both familiar and original music. Their CDs can be ordered through the Bilingual Journey Web site (a comprehensive resource for many Spanish language materials) at www.bilingualjourney.com/muisc.html. More songs and rhymes by Barbara Cass-Beggs can be found on the CDs at the Mother Goose on the Loose Web site (www.mgol.net/public/products.htm). Remember, do not limit yourself to these. The more exposure to different types of music, the better! The following table presents a short list of recommended CDs for children.

Author	Title	Language	Notes
Barchas, Sarah	*¡Piñata! and More! Bilingual Songs for Children*	Bilingual	High Haven Music
Cantarima	*Canciones tradicionales: Traditional Children's Songs in Spanish*	Spanish	Cantarima CDs also in Spanish and English
Del Rey, Maria	*Canciones de cuna de Latinoamerica*	Spanish	*Lullabies of Latin America*
Orozco, José Luis	*Lirica infantil* (series)	Spanish	Currently 12 volumes in this series by Arcoiris Records
Paz, Suni	*Alerta Sings: Children's Songs in Spanish and English*	Bilingual	Smithsonian
Trepsi	*Trepsi* (6 different volumes)	Spanish	Centro de estimulación y desarrollo infantil
Valeri, Michele	*Mi casa es su casa/My House Is Your House*	Bilingual	Caedmon

Chapter Resources

Barlin, Anne Lief. 1979. *Teaching Your Wings to Fly: The Nonspecialist's Guide to Movement Activities for Young Children.* Santa Monica: Goodyear.

Barlin, Anne, and Paul Barlin. 1971. *The Art of Learning through Movement.* Los Angeles: Ward Ritchie.

Bryant, P.D., M. MacLean, L. Bradley, and J. Crossland. 1990. "Rhyme and Alliteration, Phoneme Detection, and Learning to Read." *Developmental Psychology* 26, no. 3: 429–438.

Cass-Beggs, Barbara. 1978. *Your Baby Needs Music.* North Vancouver, British Columbia: Douglas & McIntyre.

———. 1981. "The Need for a Musical Environment during Babyhood." *Journal–Association for the Care of Children's Health* 9, no. 4: 132–135.

———. 1986. *Your Child Needs Music.* Mississauga, Ontario, Canada: The Frederick Harris Music Co.

———. 1991. "How Music Is First Introduced." *Ostinato* 17 (January): 120–121.

Honig, A.S. 1995. "Singing with Infants and Toddlers." *Young Children* 50, no. 5: 72–78.

———. 2005. "The Language of Lullabies." *Young Children* 60, no. 5: 30–36.

Jensen, Eric. 2000. *Music with the Brain in Mind.* San Diego: The Brain Store.

Levitan, Daniel J. 2000. "In Search of the Musical Mind." *Cerebrum* 2, no. 4 (Fall): 31–49.

MacLean, M., P. Bryant, and L. Bradley. 1987. "Rhymes, Nursery Rhymes, and Reading in Early Childhood." *Merill-Palmer Quarterly* 33, no. 3: 255–281.

Newberger, J.J. 1997. "New Brain Development Research—A Wonderful Window of Opportunity to Build Public Support for Early Childhood Education!" *Young Children* (May): 4–9. Available: www.thelittleschool.net/PDF/new%20brain%20development%20research.pdf (accessed October 14, 2009).

Peretz, I., and R. Zatorre. 2005. "Brain Organization for Music Processing." *Annual Review of Psychology* 56: 89–114.

Perret, Peter, and Janet Fox. 2004. *A Well-Tempered Mind: Using Music to Help Children Listen and Learn.* New York: Dana Press.

Weinberger, Norman M. Irvine. 1998. "The Music in Our Minds" *Educational Leadership* 56, no. 3: 36–40.

Zero to Three. 1998. *Young Children and the Arts: Making Creative Connections, A Report of the Task Force on Children's Learning and the Arts: Birth to Age Eight.* Arts Education Partnership. Washington, DC: Zero to Three.

———. 2002. *Getting in Tune: The Powerful Influence of Music on Young Children's Development.* Pamphlet. Washington, DC: Zero to Three.

———. 2002. *Zero to Three,* 23, no. 1. National Center for Infants, Toddlers, and Families. Washington, DC: Zero to Three. Available: www.zerotothree.org/site/PageServer?pagename=est_journal_index_archives (accessed November 9, 2009).

Chapter 10

Choosing Books and Using Flannel Boards

Choosing Books

The Opening Rhymes and Reads/Rimas y lectura section of Mother Goose on the Loose en Español is the only time within the program that a book is read aloud, cover to cover. While some children have a hard time keeping focused, others love this part. There are just a few simple rules concerning book selection:

- Choose books with large, colorful pictures.
- Make sure you *like* the story being read.
- Older children are a powerful influence for younger children to pay attention; choose books that will be of interest to them also.
- Don't read bilingual books in both languages. Focus on just one language at a time. For instance, you might read "Pollito pequeño" in Spanish for three weeks in a row and then read its counterpoint: the English-language version of "Chicken Little."
- Limit your use of bilingual books, and use them carefully. It is best to read in just one language or the other, instead of reading one sentence in two different languages.
- Try reading just a few pages of the book. If you can create interest, patrons are more likely to check it out and take it home.
- Use English-language books in addition to Spanish books.
- Choose books with a simple story line.
- Don't read a book with nonsense words.
- Choose books that have good vocabulary words.
- Choose books that have a clear story line.
- Choose books that include topics common between English and Spanish cultures.

The following tables provide some books from which to choose.

Libros Para Niños Pequeños (Ages 0–3) / Books for Small Children (Ages 0–3)

Author	Title	Language	English Title
Bang, Molly	*Diez, nueve, ocho*	Spanish	*Ten, Nine, Eight*
Boyton, Sandra	*Perritos*	Spanish	*Little Dogs*
Brown, Margaret Wise	*El gran granero rojo*	Spanish	*Big Red Barn*
Campbell, Rod	*¡Yo no muerdo!/I Won't Bite!*	Bilingual	
Crews, Donald	*Tren de carga*	Spanish	*Freight Train*
Gliori, Debi	*Siempre te querré*	Spanish	*No Matter What*
Grossman, Virginia	*Diez conejitos*	Spanish	*Ten Little Rabbits*
Guy, Ginger		English	*Siesta*
Hague, Michael	*Mamá Gansa: Una colección de rimas infantiles clásicas*	Spanish	
Hill, Eric	*¿Dónde está Spot?*	Spanish	*Where's Spot?*
Kalan, Robert	*¡Salta, ranita salta!*	Spanish	*Jump, Frog, Jump!*
Martin, Bill	*Oso pardo, oso pardo, ¿que ves ahí?*	Spanish	*Brown Bear, Brown Bear, What Do You See?*
Mora, Pat	*¡Ven, gatita, ven!*	Bilingual	*Here, Kitty, Kitty!*
Orozco, José Luis	*Diez deditos*	Bilingual	*Ten Little Fingers*
Packard, Mary	*¿Dónde está Jake?*	Spanish	*Where Is Jake?*
Peck, Merle	*¡Dénse vuelta! Una canción de cuentos*	Bilingual	*Roll Over! A Counting Song*
Pérez, Amada Irma	*Nana's Big Surprise/Nana, ¡que sorpresa!*	Bilingual	
Robleda, Magarita	*Sueños*	Spanish	
Schiller, Pam, Rafael Lara-Alecio, and Beverly J. Irby	*Bilingual Book of Rhymes, Songs, Stories, and Fingerplays*	Bilingual	

Libros Para Niños (Ages 3–5) / Books for Children (Ages 3–5)

Author	Title	Language	English Title
Aardema, Verna	*Borreguita y el coyote*	Spanish	*Borreguita and the Coyote*
Carlson, Nancy	*¡Me gusto como soy!*	Spanish	*I Like Me!*
Cooper, Helen	*Hay un oso en el cuarto oscuro*	Spanish	*The Bear Under the Stairs*
Freeman, Don	*Corduroy*	Spanish	*Corduroy*
Geeslin, Campbell		English	*On Ramon's Farm*
Gorbachev, Valeri	*Ricitos de Oro y los tres Osos*	Spanish	*Goldilocks and the Three Bears*
Hest, Amy	*Un beso de buenas noches*	Spanish	*Kiss Good Night*
Hutchins, Pat	*Llaman a la puerta*	Spanish	*The Doorbell Rang*
Janovitz, Marilyn	*¡Cuidado, pajarito!*	Spanish	*Look Out, Bird!*
Keats, Erza Jack	*Silba por Willie*	Spanish	*Whistle for Willie*
Kellogg, Steven	*Pollita pequeñita*	Spanish	*Chicken Little*
Laínez, René C.	*Playing Lotería: El juego de la Lotería*	Bilingual	
MacDonald, Margaret		Bilingual	*Conejito: A Folktale From Panama*
Martinez, Alejandro Cruz	*La mujer que Brillaba aún más que el sol*	Bilingual	*The Woman Who Outshone the Sun*
Masurel, Claire	*Diez perros en la tienda*	Spanish	*Ten Dogs in the Window*
Numeroff, Laura	*Si le das una galletita a un ratón*	Spanish	*If You Give a Mouse a Cookie*
Paul, Ann Whitford		English	*Mañana, Iguana*
Polette, Keith	*Isabel y el coyote hambriento*	English	*Isabel and the Hungry Coyote*
Rohmer, Harriet	*El sombrero del tío Nacho*	Bilingual	*Uncle Nacho's Hat*
Sierra, Judy	*Don't Let the Tiger Get You*	Bilingual	*Multicultural folktales*

Libros Para Niños (Ages 3–5) / Books for Children (Ages 3–5) *(continued)*			
Author	**Title**	**Language**	**English Title**
Sierra, Judy	*The Goat in the Chile Patch*	Bilingual	*Multicultural folktales*
Simont, Marc	*El perro vagabundo*	Spanish	*Stray Dog*
Starr, Meg	*El día más feliz de Alicia*	Spanish	*Alicia's Happy Day*
Torres, Leyla	*Gorrión del metro*	Spanish	*Subway Sparrow*
Walsh, Ellen Stoll	*Cuenta de raton*	Spanish	*Mouse Count*
Yolen, Jane	*¿Cómo cuentan hasta diez los dinosaurios?*	Spanish	*How Do Dinosaurs Count to Ten?*

Web Sites

A few libraries provide online guides to Spanish-language materials. Particularly helpful is the Resources for Librarians Web site of the Texas State Library and Archives Commission at www.tsl.state.tx.us/ld/pubs/bilingual/bib.html.

More English-Language Books

> *The Baby Goes Beep*, by Rebecca O'Connell
> *Big Fat Hen*, by Keith Baker
> *Freight Train*, by Donald Crews
> *I Love Trains!*, by Philemon Sturges
> *I Can Do It Too!* by Karen Baicker
> *Jump Like a Frog*, by Kate Burns
> *Look Book*, by Tana Hoban
> *Maisy Goes to Bed*, by Lucy Cousins
> *My Car*, by Byron Barton
> *Peek-a-Boo . . . Who?* by Sims Taback
> *Please Baby, Please*, by Spike Lee
> *Ten Little Fingers*, by Anne Kubler
> *Tip, Tip, Dig, Dig*, by Emma Garcia
> *The Wheels on the Bus*, by Paul Zelinsky
> *Whose Feet?* by Jeanette Rowe

Using a Flannel Board

Flannel board activities help children focus their attention, provide concrete images for spoken concepts or objects, and help children develop visual learning skills. Seeing different illustrations for the same rhyme introduces children to abstract concepts (e.g., one idea can be expressed visually in different ways). Using pieces that represent the work of children's illustrators (e.g., using illustrations that have been cut out from discarded books) introduces children and their parents to the beautiful artwork accessible in books.

Using pieces on a flannel board makes your job much easier. Flannel board pieces that represent a rhyme or activity also serve as a reminder of the rhyme that comes next while you are actually presenting your program. To keep your program running smoothly, make a pile of all the materials in the order in which they will be used on a shelf inside the easel. Place sticky notes in books to indicate illustrations that match particular rhymes. Stack these books, the relevant flannel board pieces, cards with developmental tips, and notes with any other information on the shelf in the order in which they will be used. Thus, the piece at the top of the pile will be your reminder of what activity to do next.

There are many different types of pieces. Commercial flannel pieces are readily available, but often they do not have a "warm" feeling to them. One exception is flannel pieces made by Artfelt, which come with an extensive list of rhymes and suggestions in both Spanish and English.

Homemade flannel board pieces are great! Felt is very easy to cut, you can write on it with permanent marker, and, as long as you use tacky glue, it will stick to paper or fabric. Try designing your own flannel board pieces! Or, ask a talented artist on the library staff or in the community to use a black permanent marker to draw outlines of certain characters or scenes on some felt, and you can simply cut them out.

Flannel board templates are provided later in this chapter. Make your own pieces by copying them or printing them from the digital files on the CD-ROM; you can use a copy machine to resize the templates to your preferred dimensions or paste the images into a Word document and resize the images before printing. Staple the black-and-white copy to a piece of felt, and cut along the outline. Use a permanent marker to fill in the details.

If you have a good relationship with a local school, you may want to ask the art teacher if her students would be willing to design and donate one flannel board piece each to the library. You may receive some very creative and imaginative ones!

Another easy suggestion is to use actual illustrations from books. Instead of discarding pictures books that have some torn pages, ripped bindings, or scribbles, look to see if any of the illustrations would make good flannel board pieces. Cut them out and attach them to felt using tacky glue. You may want to mention the original source and the illustrator's name when using others' pictures for your flannel board pieces. After seeing one particular turtle illustration as a flannel board character in the library program for a few weeks in a row, young children will squeal with delight when they recognize that same turtle illustration in a nursery rhyme book that their family has borrowed from the library.

Here are a few tips to keep in mind when making flannel board pieces:

- Make sure your pieces are large enough to be seen. Any piece smaller than your fist is too small!
- Although Velcro sticks to felt, it is not recommended for use on the flannel board, because it often "pills" up the felt, leaving the flannel board looking worn.
- Use only tacky glue on your felt pieces. It can be purchased at fabric stores or in the sewing section of stores such as Kmart. When tacky glue dries, it is clear. Most other glues do not work well with felt.
- Rather than squeezing out the tacky glue, pour some on a folded piece of paper, and use a craft stick to spread it on the pieces you would like to glue.
- Decorate your characters with googly eyes, markers, fabric paints, small pom-poms, pieces of fabric, colored pencils, buttons, or anything else you can think of! However, don't use glitter glue, because it may make your pieces too heavy and takes a very long time to dry.
- Although you may want to use layers of felt when making your characters, more than four layers of felt is too heavy and may result in the piece falling off of the flannel board.
- Don't make your pieces too thin, because they may rip; give them a background to ensure durability. For instance, let's say you've cut out an animal with a long, thin tail. When using that piece on its own, you run the risk of the tail coming off. By gluing that piece to a larger piece of felt (perhaps onto a large oval of different-colored felt as a background), you will create a piece that is esthetically pleasing, easy to handle, and sturdier.
- More is less! Create only a minimum number of pieces per rhyme. One or two pieces to represent an entire poem are generally plenty! Having too many pieces is unwieldy for the presenter and visually confusing for the audience.
- If you are using actual illustrations from discarded books, you may want to laminate them before attaching the felt backing.

Once your pieces are made, store them in a stiff folder. Keep the folder in the storage bin that you use during your programs. When you are setting up for a program, the pieces you need will be right there! When you are cleaning up from a program, make sure to take the pieces out of the storage bin where they have been dropped along with books, puppets, and instruments that you have used during your program. Put them back in the folder, and place the folder back in the bin. If pieces are not kept in a folder, they can get permanently creased. In addition to looking worn, creases make it harder for a piece to stay on the flannel board.

Recommended Flannel Board Resources

Artfelt

www.artfelt.net/warehouse/front.htm
Artfelt sells charming characters that are wonderful for nursery rhyme programs. Rhyme suggestions in both English and Spanish are included.

NASCO

www.enasco.com/artsandcrafts
NASCO sells craft supplies such as tacky glue, wiggly eyes, and colorful felt pieces for a good price.

Mother Goose on the Loose en Español Flannel Board Patterns

Templates (illustrations by Celia Yitzhak) for the following flannel board characters are included at the end of this chapter for ease of photocopying and also on the accompanying CD-ROM:

Template 1: Hen and Chicks—for "Los pollitos dicen"
Template 2: Bate Chocolate—a few different pieces for making chocolate for the "Chocolate" rhyme
Template 3: Elephant and Spider Web—for "Un elefante se balanceaba"
Template 4: Spider—for "La araña grandotota"
Template 5: Turtle and Shell—for "Buenas días, Señora Tomasa" and "La tortuga Tomasa"
Template 6: Spanish Mother Goose—for "La vieja Mamá Gansa"
Template 7: Knee Bounces—a generic picture for use with all knee bounce rhymes
Template 8: Teresa, the Queen—for "Teresa, la Marquesa"
Template 9: Jack Be Nimble and Candlestick—for jumping over the candlestick
Template 10: Humpty Dumpty and Wall—for "Jamti Damti"

Print Resources

Aardema, Verna. 1991. *Borreguita and the Coyote/Borreguita y el coyote*. New York: Knopf/Random House.
Arena, Jill, and Rene Colato Lainez. 2005. *Playing Loteria/El juego de la loteria*. Flagstaff: Luna Rising.
Baker, Keith. 1999. *Big Fat Hen*. London: Voyager.
Bang, Molly, and Clarita Kohen. 1997. *Diez, Nueve, Ocho* (Spanish Edition). New York: Greenwillow Books.
Barton, Byron. 1994. *Trains*. New York: HarperFestival.
Boynton, Sandra. 2004. *Doggies/Perritos* (Spanish Version). New York: Libros Para Niños.

Brown, Margaret Wise. 1996. *Big Red Barn* (Spanish Edition): *El gran granero rojo*. ABRIL: Rayo.

Burns, Kate. 1999. *Jump Like a Frog!* (Animal Mimics). New York: Sterling.

Campbell, Rod. 2001. *I Won't Bite!/¡Yo no muerdo!* (Spanish Edition). Scarborough, Ontario, Canada: Pan Asian Publications.

Carlson, Nancy, and Dolores Koch. 1997. *I Like Me!/¡Me gusta como soy!* New York: Viking.

Cohn, Robert (author), and Aida E. Kalan (translator). 1994. *Jump, Frog, Jump!/¡Salta, ranita, salta!* (Spanish Edition). New York: Mulberry Books.

Cooper, Helen. 1999. *There Is a Bear Under the Stairs/Hay un oso en el cuarto oscuro* (Spanish Edition). Barcelona: Editorial Juventud.

Cousins, Lucy. 1990. *Maisy Goes to Bed*. New York: Little, Brown.

Crews, Donald. 2003. *Freight Train/Tren de carga*. ABRIL: Rayo.

Freeman, Don. 2008. *Corduroy 40th Anniversary Edition*. New York: Viking Juvenile.

Garcia, Emma. 2007. *Tip, Tip, Dig, Dig*. London: Boxer Books.

Geeslin, Campbell, and Petra Mathers. 1998. *On Ramon's Farm: Five Tales of Mexico*. New York: Atheneum/Anne Schwartz Books.

Gliori, Debi, and Concha Cardennoso. 2000. *No Matter What /Â siempre te querre*. Barcelona: Timun Mas.

Gorbachev, Valeri, and Antreasyan Agustin. 2003. *Ricitos de oro y los tres osos*. New York: Ediciones Norte-Sur.

Guy, Ginger Foglesong. 2005. *Siesta*. New York: Greenwillow Books.

Hague, Michael. 1996. *Mamá Gansa*. Leon: Editorial Everest.

Hest, Amy, Anita Jeram, and Esther Rubio. 2001. *Un beso de buenas noches*. New York: Lectorum Publications.

Hill, Eric. 1980. *Where's Spot?/¿Donde esta Spot?* New York: Putnam.

Hoban, Tana. 1997. *Look Book*. New York: Greenwillow Books.

Hutchins, Pat. 1994. *The Doorbell Rang /Llaman a la puerta* (Spanish Edition). New York: Mulberry Books.

Irby, Beverly J., Rafael Lara-Alecio, and Pam Schiller. 2004. *The Bilingual Book of Rhymes, Songs, Stories, and Fingerplays/El libro bilingue de rimas, canciones, cuentos y juegos*. Beltsville, MD: Gryphon House.

Janovitz, Marilyn, and Alis Alejandro. 1997. *Look Out, Bird/Cuidado pajarito* (Spanish Edition). New York: North-South Books.

Kaminski, Robert, and Judy Sierra. *Multicultural Folktales: Stories to Tell Young Children*. Phoenix: Oryx Press, 1991.

Keats, Ezra Jack. 1992. *Whistle for Willie/Silbale a Willie*. New York: Scholastic.

Kellogg, Steven. 1993. *Pollita pequeñita/Chicken Little* (Spanish Edition). León, Spain: Editorial Everest.

Kubler, Annie. 2003. *Ten Little Fingers*. New York: Child's Play International.

Laden, Nina. 2000. *Peek-a-Who? Board Book*. San Francisco: Chronicle Books.

Lee, Spike, and Tonya Lewis Lee. 2006. *Please, Baby, Please*. New York: Aladdin.

MacDonald, Margaret Read, and Geraldo Valerio. 2006. *Conejito: A Folktale from Panama*. Little Rock: August House.

Martin, Bill. 1998. *Brown Bear, Brown Bear, What Do You See?/Oso pardo, oso pardo, ¿qué ves ahí?* New York: Henry Holt.

Martinez, Alejandro Cruz, Harriet Rohmer, David Schecter, and Rosalma Zubizarreta-Ada. 1991. *The Woman Outshone the Sun/La mujer que brillaba aún más que el sol.* San Francisco: Children's Book Press.

Masurel, Claire, Pamela Paparone, and Elena Moro. 2000. *Ten Dogs in the Window/Diez perros en la tienda* (Spanish Edition). New York: North-South/Night Sky Books.

Mora, Pat. 2008. *Here, Kitty, Kitty!/¡Ven, gatita, ven!* (My Family: Mi familia). ABRIL: Rayo.

Numeroff, Laura Joffe, and Felicia Bond. 1995. *If You Give a Mouse a Cookie/Si le das una galletita a un raton* (Spanish Edition). New York: HarperCollins.

Orozco, José Luis. 1997. *Ten Little Fingers/Diez deditos.* New York: Scholastic.

Packard, Mary, and C.S. Ewing. 1990. *Where Is Jake?/¿Donde esta Jake?* (Spanish Edition). Chicago: Children's Book Press.

Paul, Ann Whitford, and Ethan Long. 2004. *Mañana, Iguana.* New York: Holiday House.

Peck, Merle. 2008. *Roll Over! A Counting Song/¡Dénse vuelta! Una canción de cuentos.* New York: Clarion.

Pérez, Amada Irma. 2007. *Nana's Big Surprise/Nana, ¡qué sorpresa!* Chicago: Children's Book Press.

Polette, Keith, and Esther Szegedy. 2004. *Isabel and the Hungry Coyote/Isabel y el coyote hambriento.* Green Bay: Raven Tree Press.

Rohmer, Harriet, and Reisberg Veg. 1989. *Uncle Nacho's Hat/El sombrero del tío Nacho.* San Francisco: Children's Book Press.

Rowe, Jeanette. 1999. *Whose Feet?* Boston: Little, Brown.

Simont, Marc. 2003. *Stray Dog/El perro vagabundo* (Spanish Edition). New York: Rayo/HarperCollins.

Starr, Meg, Ying-Hwa Hu, Cornelius Van Wright, and María A. Fiol. 2002. *El día mas feliz de Alicia* (Spanish Edition). New York: Star Bright Books.

Sturges, Philemon. 2003. *I Love Trains!* New York: HarperCollins.

Torres, Leyla. 1993. *Subway Sparrow/Gorrion del metro.* New York: Mirasol/Libros Juveniles.

Trevino, Rose Sertuche. 2009. *Read Me a Rhyme in Spanish and English/Léame una rima en Español e Ingles.* Chicago: American Library Association.

Wadham, Tim. 1999. *Programming with Latino Children's Materials.* New York: Neal-Schuman.

Walsh, Ellen Stoll, and Gerardo Cabello. 1992. *Mouse Count/Cuenta ratones.* Mexico City: Fondo de Cultura Económica.

Yolan, Jane, and Mark Teague. 2004. *How Do Dinosaurs Count to Ten?/¿Como cuentan haste diez los dinosaurios?* (Spanish Edition). New York: Scholastic.

Zelinsky, Paul. 1990. *The Wheels on the Bus.* New York: Dutton Juvenile.

Web Resources

"El día de los niños/El día de los libros (Childrens' Day/Book Day): A Celebration of Childhood and Bilingual Literacy." Texas State Library and Archive Commission. Available: www.tsl.state.tx.us/ld/projects/ninos/profres.html (accessed October 14, 2009). This resource provides a bibliography of books, Web sites, and recommended lists of Spanish materials.

Template 1: Hen and Chicks

Template 2: Bate Chocolate

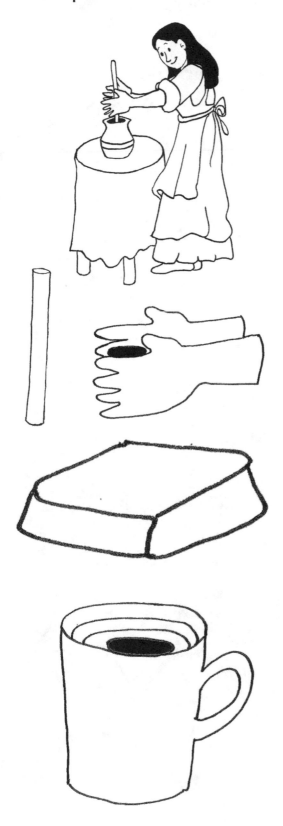

Template 3: Elephant and Spider Web

Template 4: Spider

Template 5: Turtle and Shell

Template 6: Spanish Mother Goose

Template 7: Knee Bounces

Template 8: Teresa, the Queen

Template 9: Jack Be Nimble and Candlestick

Template 10: Humpty Dumpty and Wall

PART III

Personalizing Mother Goose on the Loose en Español

Chapter 11

Planning and Customizing Programs and Weekly Activities

As mentioned in Chapter 6, when working with a Spanish-speaking partner, both presenters can sit on either side of the flannel board. Both presenters should recite the rhymes and do the corresponding movements at all times. Even if you do not speak Spanish, it is essential that you recite the rhymes together with your partner. It makes sense for you to speak softly so that your partner's voice can cover up your imperfect pronunciations and random words. However, the message given to the program participants is that you are trying and that you consider their language important. Doing this and showing your imperfect Spanish skills will make you more approachable. Spanish speakers with very limited English who might not ordinarily try to communicate with an English speaker may feel safe conversing with you. By being willing to make language mistakes with them, you are making it clear that it is fine for them to also make language mistakes with you.

The most important part of this, however, is to enjoy yourself. Don't sweat the small stuff. If you worry about your mistakes, you might project an aura of discomfort. And above all, you want to be approachable.

So, have fun while stumbling along, enjoy the cadency and richness of this new language. You will be surprised how quickly you will be able to pick up the words and how appreciative your audience will be when you sing along with them. And remember, you are not a performer at the library who has been commissioned to entertain your audience. Rather, you are a *facilitator*, and your main role is to model desired activities, encouraging parents and caregivers to practice those activities individually with their children.

Before you start planning your first program, make a list of the songs and rhymes that you know and enjoy. List up to ten rhymes for each Mother Goose on the Loose program category, and assign a number to each rhyme. If they fit into more than one category, cross-reference them by using parentheses. Once you have created your list, look at the planning sheet provided in Figure 11.1, and fill in the blank spaces with songs you know.

The Program Planning Worksheet

Program planning sheets for creating your own Mother Goose on the Loose en Español program are provided in Figures 11.1 and 11.2. These forms make planning very easy. The planning sheets feature mandatory, suggested, and open fields; Figure 11.1 is fully customizable, and Figure 11.2 is a prescripted plan based on the program presented in Chapter 8 and on the accompanying CD-ROM.

To customize your program using either planning sheet:

- You must use the materials listed as "mandatory." These are included on both planning sheets.
- For blank spaces on Figure 11.1, you may choose from the "suggested" materials included on Figure 11.2. These rhymes appear in parentheses to indicate that they are only suggestions and that you may replace them with a choice of your own.
- You are free to fill in any choice under "open," and Figure 11.2 offers some suggestions.

To plan your first program:

1. Make a photocopy of the Program Planning Worksheet and fill in the blanks with the songs and rhymes that you and your partner have chosen for your first program. Make sure that the majority of the material is in Spanish, although some can be in English.
2. The mandatory materials that need to be consistently repeated are already filled into the corresponding blanks.
3. Suggested materials that I recommend are provided in the Sample Program Plan, but feel free to replace them with selections preferred by you and your partner.
4. The open materials for you and your partner to choose are left blank. Fill in the blanks with the songs, rhymes, and stories you prefer.
5. Add one or two developmental tips (for examples, see Chapter 8's program plan and the suggestions in Chapter 14). You have just planned your first customized Mother Goose on the Loose en Español program!
6. Create a folder on your computer called "MGOL." Download the planning sheets from the CD-ROM onto your computer, saving them in this folder using the date of your first program as the title of the document. Fill in the script that you have created with your partner.

To plan your entire series of programs:

1. Open your Program Planning Worksheet from the first program (the document with the date of your first program as its title), and save it with the date of your second session.

2. Change five or six things. These can include songs, rhymes, the book to read aloud, instruments used, flannel board pieces or illustrations to accompany rhymes, or rhyme activities (e.g., you might change a rhyme you have done as a fingerplay the previous week to be done as a knee bounce or standing rhyme for the next session). *To easily see what you have changed, highlight your changes or type them using a different font. Remember, the 20 percent change translates into changing about five or six things only.*

3. Change your developmental tips. Remember that these tips can be used anywhere in the session, depending on the rhymes and activities you choose.

4. Save the document with the date of your next planned session. Voilá! Your program is ready.

5. Repeat each week. After a few weeks, you may decide to bring back items that were taken out of earlier programs.

6. Do this week after week and you will have a complete series of Mother Goose on the Loose en Español sessions. Planning time is kept to a minimum, repetition and ritual are built in, and you are ensured a high-quality program!

Keep in mind:

- For revisions, it is okay to use one rhyme four weeks in a row, drop it for four weeks, and then reintroduce it. Or, you can sing one rhyme in the opening sequence, and then move it to another part of the session.

- Some rhymes are already filled in with the ones that I highly recommend for use in those places, at those times. Of course you can choose to replace them, but in order to have the best possible program, I recommended that you learn those rhymes (many of them by Barbara Cass-Beggs) and include them in most (if not all) programs. Keep the structure, and remember that 80 percent repetition is the key to this program (changing about five or six things per week). After your first ten weeks, you can reprint the sheets and start all over, using your last program as a base for keeping the 80 percent repetition. *If you can't think of enough rhymes for a category, don't worry! Just start with what you already know* (and learn more by listening to the accompanying CD).

The following list presents the songs in the order that they appear in the prescribed program provided in Figure 11.2. This type of outline can be used as a quick guide, a reminder for the rhymes you have chosen and their place in the program. These rhymes are also on the accompanying CD, in the same order. *(continued, p. 116)*

Figure 11.1: Program Planning Worksheet

MOTHER GOOSE ON THE LOOSE EN ESPAÑOL

Week No.: _____

Segment 1: Welcoming Remarks/Bienvenidos

Segment 2: Opening Rhymes and Reads/Rimas y lectura

- Mandatory general rhyme:
  "We're So Happy That Everyone Is Here"/"Estamos contentos"
- Mandatory general rhyme:
  "Old Mother Goose"/"La vieja Mamá Gansa"
- General rhyme:

  _____

- General rhyme:

  _____

- Open choice book for reading aloud:

  _____

- Open choice rhyme:

  _____

Segment 3: Body Rhymes/Rimas del cuerpo

- Head rhyme:

  _____

- Head or finger or hand rhyme:

  _____

- Open choice finger or hand rhyme:

  _____

- Open choice finger, hand, torso, leg, or foot patting or tickle rhyme:

  _____

- Open choice torso, leg, foot patting, tickle, or knee bounce rhyme:

  _____

- Knee bounce rhyme:

  _____

- Knee bounce rhyme:

  _____

Figure 11.1: Program Planning Worksheet *(continued)*

- Optional additional knee bounce:

  _____

Segment 4: Rum Pum Pum Drum Sequence/Sequencia de "rum pum peta"

- Mandatory activity:
  Rum Pum Pum"/"Rum pum peta"

Segment 5: Standing-Up Activities/Actividades al pararse

- Standing rhyme:

  _____

- Open choice standing rhyme:

  _____

- Optional choice standing rhyme:

  _____

- Optional standing rhyme (to direct people to sit down):

  _____

Segment 6: Animals!/¡Animales!

- Mandatory animal rhyme (to use with book illustrations):
  "I Went to Visit the Farm"/"Fui a visitar la granja"
- Mandatory animal rhyme (to use with puppets or toys):
  "When the [Cats] Get Up in the Morning"/"Cuando los [gatos] se despiertan"
- Open choice optional animal rhyme:

  _____

- Optional animal rhyme (to use with one stuffed animal):

  _____

Segment 7: Musical Instruments and Props/Instrumentos musicales y accesorios

- Mandatory instrument rhyme:
  "We Ring Our Bells Together"/"Toquemos campanillas" (if using bells)
- Open choice instrument rhyme:

  _____

- Open choice instrument rhyme or activity:

  _____

Figure 11.1: Program Planning Worksheet *(continued)*

- Optional instrument rhyme:

  _____

- Mandatory instrument rhyme:
  "Bells Away"/"Entréguenlas" (if using bells)

Repeat instrument sequence once with a different instrument or choose to use props such as colored scarves (see following).

- Mandatory scarf rhyme:
  "Wind, Oh Wind"/"Viento, ay viento"
- Scarf rhyme:

  _____

- Open choice scarf rhyme or activity:

  _____

- Optional scarf rhyme and activity:

  _____

- Mandatory scarf rhyme:
  "Scarves Away"/"Entréguenlos, entréguenlos"

Segment 8: Lullabies/Cancioncitas

- Open choice lullaby:

  _____

Segment 9: Interactive Rhymes/Rimas interactivas

- Interactive rhyme:

  _____

- Optional additional interactive rhyme:

  _____

Segment 10: Closing Section/Despedida

- Mandatory closing rhyme:
  "Can You Kick with Two Feet?"/"¿Puedes patear con dos pies?"
- Mandatory closing rhyme:
  "We're So Happy That Everyone Is Here"/"Estamos contentos"
- Closing phrase:

  _____

Figure 11.2: Sample Program Plan

Mother Goose on the Loose en Español
Week No.: _____

Segment 1: Welcoming Remarks/Bienvenidos

Segment 2: Opening Rhymes and Reads/Rimas y lectura

- Mandatory general rhyme:
  "We're So Happy That Everyone Is Here"/"Estamos contentos"
- Mandatory general rhyme:
  "Old Mother Goose"/"La vieja Mamá Gansa"
- General rhyme:
  ("Good Morning, Mrs. Tomasa"/"Buenos días, Señora Tomasa")
- General rhyme:
  ("Little Chicks Are Singing"/"Los pollitos dicen")
- Open choice book for reading aloud:
  (*Where's Spot?*/*¿Donde está Spot?*)
- Open choice rhyme:
  ("We Hit the Floor Together"/"Pegamos el piso juntos")

Segment 3: Body Rhymes/Rimas del cuerpo

- Head rhyme:
  ("Where Is My Head?"/"¿Dónde está mi cabeza?")
- Head or finger or hand rhyme:
  ("Fingers Like to Wiggle Waggle"/"Tengo manitas")
- Open choice finger or hand rhyme:
  ("Little Tortillas for Mama/Potatoes and Potatoes"/"Tortillitas para mamá/Papas y papas")
- Open choice finger, hand, torso, leg, or foot patting or tickle rhyme:
  ("The Eency Weency Spider/Great Big Spider"/"La araña pequiñita/grandotota")
- Open choice torso, leg, foot patting, tickle rhyme, or knee bounce:
  ("This Is the Way the Ladies Ride"/"Así al caballo montan las damas")
- Knee bounce rhyme:
  ("Giddy-Up My Horse"/"Ándale caballo")

Figure 11.2: Sample Program Plan *(continued)*

- Knee bounce rhyme:
  ("Jack and Jill"/"Juan y Juana")
- Optional additional knee bounce:
  ("Mother and Father and Uncle John"/"Mamá, papa, y el tío Juan")

Segment 4: Rum Pum Pum Drum Sequence/Sequencia de "rum pum peta"

- Mandatory activity:
  "Rum Pum Pum"/"Rum pum peta"

Segment 5: Standing-Up Activities/Actividades al pararse

- Standing rhyme:
  ("And We Walk and We Walk and We Walk"/"Y caminamos")
- Open choice standing rhyme:
  ("The Chirimbolo Game"/"El juego chirimbolo")
- Optional choice standing rhyme:
  ("Stir It, Stir the Chocolate"/"Bate, bate, chocolate")
- Optional standing rhyme (to direct people to sit down):
  ("Handy Spandy")

Segment 6: Animals!/¡Animales!

- Mandatory animal rhyme (to use with book illustrations):
  "I Went to Visit the Farm"/"Fui a visitar la granja"
- Mandatory animal rhyme (to use with puppets or toys):
  "When the [Cats] Get Up in the Morning"/"Cuando los [gatos] se despiertan"
- Open choice optional animal rhyme:
  ("One Elephant Went Out to Play"/"Un elefante se balanceaba")
- Optional animal rhyme (to use with one stuffed animal):
  ("Hickory Dickory Dare"/"El cochinito")

Segment 7: Musical Instruments and Props/Instrumentos musicales y accesorios

- Mandatory instrument rhyme:
  "We Ring Our Bells Together"/"Toquemos campanillas"
- Open choice instrument rhyme:
  ("Are You Sleeping, Brother John?"/"Martinillo")
- Open choice instrument rhyme or activity:
  ([Ring bells] along to music)

Figure 11.2: Sample Program Plan *(continued)*

- Optional instrument rhyme:
  ("Teresa, the Queen"/"Teresa, la marquesa")
- Mandatory instrument rhyme:
  "Bells Away"/"Entréguenlas"

Repeat instrument sequence once with a different instrument or choose to use props such as colored scarves (see following).

- Mandatory scarf rhyme:
  "Wind, Oh Wind"/"Viento, ay viento"
- Scarf rhyme:
  ("Peek-a-Boo"/"Peek-a-boo")
- Open choice scarf rhyme or activity:
  ("This Is the Way We Wash"/"Así vamos a lavarnos")
- Optional scarf rhyme and activity:
  ("De colores"; play this song from a CD and ask everyone to wave their scarves along with the music)
- Mandatory scarf rhyme:
  "Scarves Away"/"Entréguenlos, entréguenlos"

Segment 8: Lullabies/Cancioncitas

- Open choice lullaby:
  ("Twinkle, Twinkle"/"Estrellita")

Segment 9: Interactive Rhymes/Rimas interactivas

- Interactive rhyme:
  ("Jack Be Nimble"/"¡Juan alerta!")
- Optional additional interactive rhyme:
  ("Humpty Dumpty"/"Jamti Damti")

Segment 10: Closing Section/Despedida

- Mandatory closing rhyme:
  "Can You Kick with Two Feet?"/"¿Puedes patear con dos pies?"
- Mandatory closing rhyme:
  "We're So Happy That Everyone Is Here"/"Estamos contentos"
- Closing phrase:
  ("Bye everybody!"/"¡Adios a todos!")

1. **Welcoming Remarks/Bienvenidos** ☺#3
    Introduce yourself
    Children this age don't sit perfectly still
    Set boundaries
    Explain how the program works

2. **Opening Rhymes and Reads/Rimas y lectura** ☺#4
    Song: "We're So Happy That Everyone Is Here"/"Estamos contentos"
    Flannel board: "Old Mother Goose"/"La vieja Mamá Gansa"
    Puppet: ("Good Morning, Mrs. Tomasa"/"Buenos días, Señora Tomasa")
    Illustration with rhyme: ("Little Chicks Are Singing"/"Los pollitos dicen")
    Book: (*Where's Spot?*/*¿Donde está Spot?*)
    Song: ("We Hit the Floor Together"/"Pegamos el piso juntos")

3. **Body Rhymes/Rimas del cuerpo** ☺#5
    Head: ("Where Is My Head?"/"Dónde está mi cabeza?")
    Fingers: ("Fingers Like to Wiggle Waggle"/"Tengo manitas")
    Hands: ("Little Tortillas for Mama/Potatoes and Potatoes"/"Tortillitas para mamá/ Papas y papas")
    Song: ("The Eency Weency Spider/Great Big Spider"/"La araña pequiñita/ grandotota")
    Knee bounces: ("This Is the Way the Ladies Ride"/"Así al caballo montan las damas")
    ("Giddy-Up My Horse!"/"Ándale caballo")
    ("Jack and Jill"/"Juan y Juana")
    ("Mother and Father and Uncle John"/"Mamá, papá, y el tío Juan")

4. **Rum Pum Pum Drum Sequence/Sequencia de "rum pum peta"** ☺#6
    "Rum Pum Pum"/"Rum pum peta"

5. **Standing-Up Activities/Actividades al pararse** ☺#7
    ("And We Walk and We Walk and We Walk"; "Y caminemos")
    ("The Chirimbolo Game"; "El juego chrimbolo")
    ("Stir It, Stir the Chocolate"; "Bate, bate, chocolate")
    ("Handy Spandy")

6. **Animals!/¡Animales!** ☺#8
    Show book illustrations: "I Went to Visit the Farm One Day"/"Fui a visitar la granja"
    With puppets: "When the [Cats] Get Up in the Morning"/"Cuando los [gatos] se despiertan"

("One Elephant Went Out to Play"/"Un elefante se balanceaba")
Pig puppet: ("Hickory Dickory Dare"/"El cochinito")

7. **Musical Instruments and Props/Instrumentos musicales y accesorios** ☉#9, #10
    Bells: "We Ring Our Bells Together"/"Toquemos campanillas"
    ("Are You Sleeping, Brother John?"/"Martinillo")
    Activity: ([Ring bells] along to music)
    ("Teresa, the Queen"/"Teresa, la marquesa")
    "Bells Away"/"Entréguenlas"
    Scarves: "Wind, Oh Wind"/"Viento viento"
    "Peek-a-Boo"/"Peek-a-boo"
    ("This Is the Way We Wash"/"Así vamos a lavar el cuello")
    Activity: (Play "De colores" and wave scarves along with music)
    "Scarves Away"/"Entréguenlos, entréguenlos"

8. **Lullabies/Cancioncitas** ☉#11
    "Twinkle, Twinkle"/"Estrellita"

9. **Interactive Rhymes/Rimas interactivas** ☉#12
    Small candlestick: ("Jack Be Nimble"/"¡Juan alerta!")
    Flannel board: ("Humpty Dumpty"/"Jamti Damti")

10. **Closing Section/Despedida** ☉#13
    "Can You Kick with Two Feet?"/"¿Puedes patear con dos pies?"
    "We're So Happy That Everyone Is Here"/"Estamos contentos"

Chapter 13 provides songs and rhymes that work well in Mother Goose on the Loose en Español. In addition to the complete lyrics to all of these songs, there are lyrics to a few other recommended songs. Titles of traditional Spanish rhymes that would work well in this setting are listed in each section under "Additional rhymes." This listing includes book title and page number where the lyrics can be found, as well as a few useful Web site addresses. The next section includes additional weekly activities to follow your actual program.

Additional Weekly Activities

There are other ways you and your partner can help participants become part of the library community. In the "free play" time after each program, choose to focus on just one part of the library, and use an impromptu script to show patrons how the library works.

Activities Inside of the Library

Explain about the Public Library

Talk about the purpose of a public library. Make it clear that anyone can come into a library, whether or not they have a library card. Access is free for all regardless of religion, race, and economic background.

Give Tours of the Library

Take your group on a tour around the library, pointing out specific areas of interest. Ask your community partner to translate anything you say and to add in anything you might leave out. Show the bathrooms, diaper changing and nursing areas if your library has them, picture book sections in both English and Spanish, the newspaper area, the video and DVD section, the CD and audiocassette area, the dictionaries, and computers. Be sure to visit every area that holds Spanish-language resources.

Explain the Function of a Public Library

Tell your families (with your partner's translation help) that your job as a public librarian is to provide information for free to the people in your community—emphasize "free." Your position is funded by taxes, and your job is providing information to people who ask for it. Therefore, you want everyone to know that you welcome their questions and hope that they will continue coming to the library, looking for information, and asking questions.

Sign Up for Library Cards

Ask your community partner to walk with the entire group up to the circulation desk. Introduce them to the circulation librarian. Show them what a library card application form looks like, and fill one out with one of the parent participants. Hand it to a preselected staff person, and wait for it to be processed. Display the new library card to everyone before giving it to the appropriate parent. After this visual explanation, your community members should become, within a short period of time, the proud owners of library cards.

Demonstrate Checking Out Books

Pantomime pulling a book off the shelf and later handing it to the circulation librarian for check out. Through your movements, show how to open the book to the label that is going to be scanned. Point out the area where the due date is stamped, and explain clearly (more than once!) about due dates and overdue fines. It is important for all families to know that although books can be borrowed for free, if they are not returned within the specified time period, a fine will be charged. Then, encourage your families to borrow materials and check them out before leaving the library that day. If your library has self-check out, repeat your visual explanation a few times until everyone seems to understand.

Sign Up for Events

If the Summer Reading Club is around the corner, this time between the end of your program and serving refreshments is a perfect time for sign up. Explain how the Summer Reading Club works (and ask your partner to translate) or hand out Spanish-language Summer Reading Club materials. Then, have your partner walk with any interested children or adults to the area where the Summer Reading Club signup is taking place. The children can be signed up on the spot, given their game board, and encouraged to get started. Adults can sign up their entire families, including school-aged children who might not be at the Mother Goose program. In addition, this informal period is a great time to advertise upcoming programs, such as concerts and films.

Demonstrate Asking Reference Questions

For this, prepare a reference question ahead of time, and give it to the person who will be on adult reference duty that day. Then, give your community partner the Spanish version of the question. Gather up your crowd, and follow your partner to the reference section. Watch as the reference question is asked; although the reference librarian does not understand Spanish, he can make it easier for people to see how he tries to understand the question and is very happy to help provide the answer. This activity can be done numerous times, using different questions or addressing other library departments.

Explain about Library Branches

If you are part of a larger library system, explain how branches work. Bring in some books from one of the other libraries, and perform a short skit with your community partner about not getting the books you want because they are not available in your local library. Through drama you can show that librarians can easily contact other branches or library system to request the materials. Be sure to dramatize a big smile when the requested materials are then presented to you by your Spanish-speaking partner. A simple verbal explanation of branches may also suffice.

In addition to using the concept of branches to show people that there is another place where they can get books, you can also stress that each branch has programs, too. And, while on the topic of branches, mention that your library card is good in any of the branches. Just because your program is being held in one library does not mean that the families can only go to that library; they are welcome to try out any of the public libraries in the area.

Another week, you may want to introduce the concept of public libraries nationwide, stressing that, although your community members may not be able to borrow materials from every library, they should be free to enter, browse a collection, ask reference questions, and attend programs in any public library in the United States.

Promote Circulation of Library Materials

Each week, encourage requests for library materials. Also, stress that the library is *free* and open many or any day of the week, even when there are not programs.

Activities Outside of the Library

You may want to talk to program participants briefly about the importance of parent–child interaction, stressing that early literacy activities are not just book related; they include singing together, playing together, and talking together. For a follow up to this, print out some of the downloadable self-evaluation sheets (in either English or Spanish) that are posted at the Washington Learning Systems' Web site (www .walearning.com/PDF/I-TSpanishChklists.pdf).

Simple activities for parents to do with their children include listening to music, singing songs, talking about nursery rhymes, looking at pictures in a book, talking about things outside, discovering print, and drawing.

Chapter 12

Feedback, Evaluation, and Celebration

Feedback

To keep accurate statistics, ask all program participants to fill out a registration form that asks for their name, their child's name, their child's age, and a few basic background questions, such as the following:

- Have you ever been to any public library before today?
- Have you been to this library before?

- Do you have a library card?
- If so, have you ever used your library card to borrow materials?

- Do you read aloud to your child?
- If so, do you read about once a year, once a month, once a week, or once a day?
- Do you sing songs with your child?
- If so, do you sing about once a month, once a week, or once a day?

- ¿Ha visitado a una biblioteca pública antes de hoy?
- ¿Ha visitado a esta biblioteca anteriormente?

- ¿Tiene usted una tarjeta de biblioteca?
- ¿Si la respuesta es sí, ha utilizado su tarjeta de biloteca para sacar materiales?

- ¿Lee usted en voz alta con su hijo/a?
- Si lo hace, ¿con qué frecuencia? ¿Una vez al mes, una vez a la semana, o una vez al día?
- ¿Canta usted canciones con su hijo/a?
- Si lo hace, ¿con qué frecuencia? ¿Una vez al mes, una vez a la semana, o una vez al día?

Date each survey, and store it in folder in the file cabinet. Every time a new person comes, have your community partner ask him or her to fill out one of these surveys, explaining that if the participant prefers, the partner will be happy to read the question aloud and write down the answers. This is essential; some of your participants may not know how to read or write in Spanish and would feel ill at ease if asked to do something that they could not. These instructions must be delivered in such a way that a person who needs this type of help does not feel embarrassed. This service can also come in handy for adults with babies in their arms; even if they know how to read and write, they might prefer to hold their baby and have someone else write down their answers. Adults should be informed that they will be asked to answer one question per week but that there is no right or wrong answer.

Before your program starts, fill a large plastic storage bin (with a cover that stays on securely unless purposefully removed by an adult!) with toys. Keep it out of the reach of the children during your program, perhaps on a shelf or behind your chair. Choose items that would work well your particular group of children. Examples include the following:

- Duplo or other building materials
- Textured balls
- Sensory tubes
- Cars and trucks
- Wooden puzzles
- Cardboard bricks
- Sorting games
- Small push toys

When the program ends, move the bin to the floor in the middle of the flannel board, open it up, and place the toys on the floor. Invite the children to play with you. Stay on the floor, and play with them! Build towers with the cardboard bricks, encourage children to place the wooden puzzle pieces in their correct places, roll the ball to enthusiastic toddlers, and show other children how to sort shapes. This type of play does not require knowledge of Spanish; speak the language you are most comfortable with while performing the actions that are understandable to children everywhere.

While you are playing, your community partner will be passing out clipboards, pencils, and pieces of paper with a question printed on it. Each week, another question can be asked. Your partner will circulate among the adults, helping those who are not comfortable reading or writing in Spanish, by asking the question to them in a quiet voice and recording their answers. If they agree, their names should be included. As they finish answering the question, the community partner can collect the papers and encourage the adults to join their children in play.

Questions should be very simple, addressing only one issue. By asking one question every week and having people write their names with their answers, you will have a way to track the growth and development of the children as well as of the family unit. These questions directly reflect the developmental tips offered in the programs. The answers can also help you determine the effectiveness of your developmental tips and may point to areas which need further reinforcement. Questions can include the following:

- Should children under the age of three be expected to sit perfectly still? Why or why not?
- What kinds of fun things can you do to help share a book with your child?

- What types of things can you find in a library?
- How can you help prepare your child to respond to the word "Stop"?
- Name a lullaby. Why is singing a lullaby to your child important?

- ¿Se debe esperar que los niños menores de tres años se sienten quietos? ¿Por qué?
- ¿Qué tipos de actividades puede hacer para convertir un libra en algo divertivo y creativo?
- ¿Qué cosas y servicios se pueden encontrar en la biblioteca?
- ¿Cómo puede prepararle a su hijo a responder a la palabra "Pare"?
- Nombre una cancioncita infantile. ¿Por qué es importante cantar a su hijo?

As the questions are finished, encourage the parents to join their children in play. When you have collected all of the answers, escort everyone to the refreshment area. Fresh fruit, cheese cubes, crackers, and juice boxes make delicious and nutritious snacks. Have tables set up with chairs all around them, and encourage participants to sit together around the same one or two tables. Take a plate of food and join them. Again, even if you don't speak Spanish, your presence among the families will be greatly appreciated.

After six months or a year, bring a laptop or set up a computer in the refreshment room. Tell the adults that you would like to hear feedback from them about the program. Invite them to come up to you one at a time (with your community partner translating) and ask them simply, "What did you think about the program"? Do not ask any leading questions, and make it clear that you want to hear all responses, both positive and negative. Listen carefully to the answers. It may give you ideas for a total renovation. Asking for comments from the parents empowers them. As they watch you type down their answers they are getting the real message that "We are in this together." You can use this information as anecdotal evidence to stress the value of certain parts of the program to your public. Questions can include the following:

- What do you think about Mother Goose on the Loose en Español?
- What would you like me to know about your experience here?
- Do you have any suggestions for this program?
- Would you recommend this program to a friend? Why or why not?

- ¿Qué opina usted de Mother Goose on the Loose en Español?
- ¿Hay algo que quiere que yo sepa acerca de su experiencia aquí?
- ¿Tiene usted alguna sugerencia para este programa?
- ¿Le recomendaría este programa a un amigo? ¿Por qué?

At the end of each program, ask parents to help clean up the refreshments (they will probably do so without even being asked). Escort them to the front of the building where they will wait for their transportation. Remind parents to keep an eye on their children as they leave the library. If the library does not have enclosed lawns, chances are that it exits directly onto the street. It is essential for the adults to keep an eye on their children to make sure they don't stray away or run into the street. If you do not feel the parents can maintain this kind of attention, stay outside and wait until everyone has been picked up.

Evaluation

After everyone is gone, with your community partner, clear away the plates and food, wipe down the tables, put away most of the chairs, and then sit down together and take notes about the program. Remember to mark down any additional information that may be relevant about the session, such as a sentence or two mentioning the one mother who seemed very distracted, the baby who whined the entire time, or the teens who can often be found in a particular corner, simply reading. Put this information in your files and use it as anecdotal evidence regarding the impact of the program when you start to reevaluate in another six months.

After a few months have passed, you may want to look over your notes from the very first program with your community partner and informally assess any changes that may have occurred. This will give you and your partner a good sense of the type of impact the program is having on the participants. In addition, these observations may provide a good starting point for an article about the program that you may want to write for a local newspaper. Excerpts from your notes may fit nicely into the library's annual report. They can also form the basis of a report for your library board. Here are questions you may want to consider:

- Has attending the program enhanced any of the relationships between parents and their children?
- Have you observed any differences in:
  - Children's ability to follow directions
  - Children's behavior in a public place
  - Parent's comfort level speaking some English
  - Family asking questions of the librarian
  - Disciplinary techniques used by parents
- Do program participants exhibit a sense of "ownership" of the library?
- Are participants singing a greater number of English songs?
- Has the number of questions participants ask and concerns they may express about their children increased?

For your reports, you may want to record program statistics:

- How many sessions were held?
- What is the total number of people who have attended sessions (all the numbers from all the sessions)?
- What is the number of unduplicated participants (the total number of people who attended the program, counting each individual only once per the entire series)?
- How many regulars are there—those who come to at least every other session?

Knowing the program's effect on library services is valuable and useful. Some questions that you may want to ask include the following:

- Was a library card issued? How many? What percentage of program participants got them?
- Were books checked out?
- Were library services used? Which ones?

You may find that your hard statistics combined with the anecdotal evidence show that your program has greatly improved the connection between the Spanish-speaking community and public library services. The hard data can be used when writing grants to request funding or to encourage the establishment of similar programs in your community.

Celebration

Young children grow and develop at an amazing rate, and it gives good cause for celebration. When you see a child mastering a song, trying a new activity that he or she has never participated in before, or advancing to the next skill level, it is always valuable to point this out to the adult. You will be forging a bond with the adult as well as strengthening their pride in their child. Possible comments include the following:

- I noticed that Billie sat on your lap for most of the program today.
- Luis might want to be an engineer when he grows up—he built an incredible bridge out of blocks before we started the program this morning.
- Today, when we were reciting "Bate chocolate," I notice that Rosa clapped her hands in perfect timing to "CHO-CO-LA-TE." Well done.
- Did you know that Lily sang all the words to one of the English songs?
- Jennifer put her bell away immediately this week when we came around with the canvas bag.

If it comes to your attention that a child has a birthday, be sure to sing "Happy Birthday" in whichever language! Encourage program participants to share happy news and celebrate through song.

PART IV

The Mother Goose on the Loose en Español Songbook, Rhymebook, and Resourcebook

Chapter 13

Song Lyrics and Rhymes with Stage Directions

Part I: Mother Goose on the Loose en Español Songs and Rhymes

This chapter begins with a list of songs and rhymes that have been used successfully in Mother Goose on the Loose en Español programs. The complete lyrics and directions for each of the numbered rhymes and songs are contained in Part II.

In Part I, the English song is listed first, followed by the Spanish title. After the numbered list in each section, a few other traditional Spanish rhymes are listed by title with a notation stating where that specific rhyme can be found—either in a book, on a Web site, or on a CD included in the Further Resources at the end of this chapter. In addition, many of the following songs can be found on the CD *Escucha y disfruta con Mama Gansa / Listen, Like, Learn with Mother Goose on the Loose*. The first section of the program should always be the Welcoming Comments (☉ #3); because this section does not have any rhymes, the following list begins with the second section.

2. Opening Rhymes and Reads/Rimas y lectura   CD Track/Source

1. "We're So Happy That Everyone Is Here"	☉ #4
2. "Estamos contentos"	☉ #4
3. "Old Mother Goose"	☉ #4
4. "La vieja Mamá Gansa"	☉ #4
5. "Good Morning, Mrs. Tomasa"	☉ #4
6. "Buenos días, Señora Tomasa"	☉ #4
7. "Little Chicks Are Singing"	☉ #4
8. "Los pollitos dicen"	☉ #4
9. "We Hit the Floor Together"	☉ #4
10. "Pegamos el piso juntos"	☉ #4
11. "Eency Weency Spider"/"Great Big Spider"	☉ #5

12. "La araña pequeñita"/"La araña grandotota"   ☉ #5
13. "Two Little Dickey Birds"
14. "Dos pajaritos"
15. "Eeeny Meeny Miney Moe"
16. "Pico pico solorico"

Additional General Rhymes

"The Wheels on the Bus"/"Las ruedas del camión"   *Diez deditos,* p. 47

3. Body Rhymes/Rimas del cuerpo   CD Track/Source

Head/Cabeza

17. "Where Is My Head?"   ☉ #5
18. "¿Dónde está mi cabeza?"   ☉ #5

Additional Head Rhymes

"Knock Knock"/"Tan Tan"   *Diez deditos,* p. 48
"My Five Senses"/"Mis cinco sentidos"   *Read Me a Rhyme,* p. 48

Fingers/Deditos

19. "Fingers Like to Wiggle Waggle"   ☉ #5
20. "A los deditos les gusta moverse"   ☉ #5
21. "Here Are Baby's Fingers"
22. "Aquí están tus deditos"

Additional Finger Rhymes

"Chico pollitos"/"Five Little Chicks"   *¡Pío peep!,* p. 12
"Pulgarcito"/"Where Is Thumbkin?"   *Diez deditos,* p. 49
"Cinco deditos"   *Mamá Gansa,* p. 11

Hands/Manitas

23. "Here Are My Hands"   ☉ #5
24. "Tengo manitas"   ☉ #5
25. "Little Tortillas for Mother/Potatoes and Potatoes"   ☉ #5
26. "Tortillitas para mamá/Papas y papas"   ☉ #5
27. "Open Them, Shut Them"
28. "Abrelas, cierraleas"
29. "Show Ten Hands and Show Ten Fingers"
30. "Dos manitas, diez deditos"

Additional Hand Rhymes

"Almendras y turrón"/"Almonds and Chestnuts"   *¡Pío peep!*, p. 16

"Palmas y palmas"   *Mamá Gansa*, p. 12

Tickle Rhymes/Rimas de cosquillas

31. "The Little Train"
32. "El trencito ya corrió"

Additional Tickle Rhymes

"Here Comes Daddy"/"Tú padre ha venido"   *Read Me a Rhyme*, p. 17

Knee Bounces/Rodillas

33. "This Is the Way the Ladies Ride"   ◉ #5
34. "Así al caballo montan las damas"   ◉ #5
35. "Giddy-Up My Horse"   ◉ #5
36. "Ándale caballo"   ◉ #5
37. "Jack and Jill"   ◉ #5
38. "Juan y Juana"   ◉ #5
39. "Mother and Father and Uncle John"
40. "Mamá, papá, y el tío Juan"

Additional Knee Bounce Rhymes

"Little White Pony"/"Caballito blanco"   *Los pollitos dicen*, p. 9

"Al paso"   *Mamá Gansa*, p. 24"

"Mrs. Blue Sky"/"La Casa de Peña"   *Diez deditos*, p. 29

Foot Patting

"Angelitos descalzos"   *¡Pio peep!*, p. 51

4. Rum Pum Pum Drum Sequence/ Secuencia de "rum pum peta"   CD Track/Source

41. "Rum Pum Pum"   ◉ #6
42. "Rum pum peta"   ◉ #6

Additional Drum Rhymes

"Al tambor"   *De colores and Other Latin American Folk Songs for Children*, Track #4

"Tambor"   *Trepsi*, Vol. 3, Track #17

5. Standing-Up Activities/Actividades al pararse   CD Track/Source

43. "And We Walk"	☉ #7
44. "Y caminamos"	☉ #7
45. "The Chirimbolo Game"	☉ #7
46. "El juego chirimbolo"	☉ #7
47. "Stir It, Stir the Chocolate"	☉ #7
48. "Bate, bate, chocolate"	☉ #7
49. "We're Marching to the Drum"	
50. "Marchamos al tambor"	
51. "Head, Shoulders, Knees, and Toes"	
52. "Cabeza, hombros, rodillas y pies"	
53. "Little Johnny Dances"	
54. "Juanito"	
55. "Handy Spandy"	
56. "Maria Antonia"	

Additional Large Motor Rhymes

"Juanito"/"Little Johnny"	*Diez deditos*, p. 18; *Lirica Infantil*, Vol. 4, Track #4
"Al corro de la patate"/"Ring around the Potato"	*Los pollitos dicen*, pp. 18–19
"Ven el puente a reparar"/"London Bridge Is Falling Down"	*Children's Nursery Rhyme Songs in Spanish*, Track #3
"La zarza azul"/"The Mulberry Bush"	*Children's Nursery Rhyme Songs in Spanish*, Track #6
"Zigu zago"/"Hokey Pokey"	*Trepsi*, Vol. 3, Track #18

6. Animals!/¡Animales!   CD Track/Source

57. "I Went to Visit the Farm"	☉ #8
58. "Fui a visitar la granja"	☉ #8
59. "When the [Cats] Get Up in the Morning"	☉ #8
60. "Cuando los [gatos] se despiertan"	☉ #8
61. "One Elephant Went Out to Play"	☉ #8
62. "Un elefante se balanceaba"	☉ #8
63. "Hickory Dickory Dare"	☉ #8
64. "El cochinito"	☉ #8

Additional Animal Rhymes

7. Musical Instruments and Props/
Instrumentos musicales y accesorios   CD Track/Source

Bells

Additional Bell Rhymes

Maracas

Additional Rhymes for Use with Maracas

"Colita de rana"   *Tortillitas para mamá*, n.p.

Rhythm Sticks

81. "We Tap Our Sticks Together"
82. "Suena los palitos"
83. "Grandfather's Clock"
84. "El reloj"
85. "Sticks Away"
86. "Palitos a la bolsa"

Additional Rhymes for Use with Rhythm Sticks

"Cinco pollitos"   *¡Pio peep!*, p. 12
"Las horas"/"The Hours"   *Diez deditos*, p. 42

Scarves

87. "Wind, Oh Wind"   ☻ #10
88. "Viento, ay viento"   ☻ #10
89. "Peek-a-Boo"   ☻ #10
90. "Peek-a-boo"   ☻ #10
91. "This Is the Way We Wash"   ☻ #10
92. "Así vamos a lavarnos"   ☻ #10
93. "Scarves Away"   ☻ #10
94. "Entréguenlos"   ☻ #10

Additional Rhymes for Use with Scarves

"Many Colors"/"De colores"   *¡Pío peep!*, pp. 22–23

8. Cancioncitas/Lullabies   CD Track/Source

95. "Twinkle, Twinkle, Little Star"   ☻ #11
96. "Estrellita dónde estás"   ☻ #11

Additional Lullabies

"El coquí/The Bullfrog"   *De colores and Other Latin American Folk Songs for Children*, Track #25

"El sol es de oro"/"The Sun's a Gold Medallion"   *¡Pío peep!*, p. 50
"Pajarito que cantas"/"Little Bird Singing"   *¡Pío peep!*, p. 550
"Los pescaditos"/"The Little Fishes"   *Tortillitas para mamá*, p. 14
"De colores"/"Oh, the Colors"   *De colores and Other Latin American Folk Songs for*

	Children, Track #13
"A dormier va la rosa"	*¡Pío peep!*, p. 52
"A la nana, nanita"	*Mamá Gansa*, p. 8
"Duermente, mi nina"	*¡Pío peep!*, p. 59

A wide variety of songs are also available on *Arrullos: Lullabies in Spanish* (Orozco, 2000).

9. Interactive Rhymes/Rimas interactivas   CD Track/Source

97. "Jack Be Nimble"	💿 #12
98. "¡Juan alerta!"	💿 #12
99. "Humpty Dumpty"	💿 #12
100. "Jamti Damti"	💿 #12

Additional Interactive Rhymes

"Brinca la tablita"/"Jump the Pole"

10. Closing Section/Despedida   CD Track/Source

101. "Can You Kick with Two Feet?"	💿 #13
102. "¿Puedes patear con dos pies?"	💿 #13

Part II: Song Lyrics and Directions

This part contains the lyrics and directions for the numbered rhymes and songs listed in Part I. The material is arranged according to program segment; within the program segments, songs are listed by number (odd numbers for English; even numbers for Spanish), and some programs are also further divided by subthemes. For ease of reference, the English and Spanish translations are presented side by side.

2. Opening Rhymes and Reads 💿 #4	**2. Rimas y lectura** 💿 #4
1 "We're So Happy That Everyone Is Here" 💿 #4	2 "Estamos contentos" 💿 #4
(Tap hands on knees while singing)	*(Dese golpecitos en las rodillas mientras que cante)*
We're so happy (3×) That everyone is here.	Estamos contentos (3×) Que todos están aquí.

We're so happy (3×)
That everyone is here.

By Barbara Cass-Beggs

Estamos contentos (3×)
Que todos están aquí.

Translation by Anne Calderón

3 "Old Mother Goose" ☉ #4

(Place Mother Goose piece on the flannel board)
Old Mother Goose
(Tap hands on legs)
When she wanted to wander
Would fly through the air
(Lift baby or move hands in arc over your head)
On a very fine gander.
(Looking at the sea, sway from side to side)

Traditional

4 "La vieja Mamá Gansa" ☉ #4

(Ponga a la vieja Mamá Gansa en la tablera de franela)
La vieja Mamá Gansa
(Dese golpecitos en las piernas)
Cuando quería pasear
Volaba por el aire
(Cargue a su bebe o mueva sus manos en forma de arco arriba de su cabeza)
Mirando el mar.
(Mirando el mar, muévase de lado a lado)

Translation by Jennifer Bown-Olmedo, Rosa Hernandez, Gilda Martinez, and Gilda Valdes

5 "Good Morning, Mrs. Tomasa" ☉ #4

Good morning, Mrs. Tomasa,
Mrs. Tomasa, Mrs. Tomasa.
Good morning, Mrs. Tomasa,
Where are you?
I'm going for a walk,
A walk, a walk.
I'm going for a walk, a walk,
And saying, "Hello."

Adapted from Barbara Cass-Beggs' "Good Morning, Mrs. Perky Bird" by Rosa Hernandez

6 "Buenos días, Señora Tomasa" ☉ #4

Buenos días, Señora Tomasa,
Señora Tomasa, Señora Tomasa.
Buenos días, Señora Tomasa,
¿Donde están usted?
Estoy tomando un paseo,
Un paseo, un paseo.
Estoy tomando un paseo, un paseo,
Y saludando "Hola."

Adapted from Barbara Cass-Beggs' "Good Morning, Mrs. Perky Bird" by Rosa Hernandez. Translation by Rosa, Hernandez, Gilda Martinez, and Gilda Valdes

7 "Little Chicks Are Singing" ☉ #4

8 "Los pollitos dicen" ☉ #4

The little chicks are singing "pío pío pío"	Los pollitos dicen pío pío pío
(Open and close hands)	*(Abra y cierre las manos)*
When they're feeling hungry	Cuando tienen hambre
(Rub tummy)	*(Frótese la barriga)*
When they're feeling cold.	Cuando tienen frío.
(Hug yourself and shiver)	*(Abrácese y tiembla)*
Mother hen is looking for some corn and wheat.	La gallina busca el maíz y el trigo.
(Make pecking motions with hands)	*(Haga gestos con las manos que parezcan picotazos)*
She gives her children food.	Les da la comida.
(Touch mouth)	*(Tóquese la boca)*
She keeps her children warm.	Les presta abrigo.
(Hug yourself)	*(Abrácese)*
The little chicks are cuddled underneath her wings.	Bajo sus alas, acurrucaditos.
(Extend bent arm in front of you and slightly rock)	*(Estire los brazos como si estuviera meciendo a un bebe)*
The little chicks are sleeping	Duermen los pollitos
(Close eyes, lean head to side on hands)	*(Cierre los ojos y acueste la cabeza para el lado sobre las manos)*
Until the morning comes.	Hasta el otro día.
Wake up!	¡Despiértense!
(Open eyes, sit up straight)	*(Abra los ojos, siéntese derecho)*
Translation to English by Anne Calderón	**Traditional**

9 "We Hit the Floor Together"   ☮ #4

We hit the floor together,
We hit the floor together,
We hit the floor together,
Because it's fun to do.

We clap our hands together, (3×)
Because it's fun to do.

We kick the floor together, (3×)
Because it's fun to do.

We smack our knees together, (3×)
Because it's fun to do.

10 Pegamos el piso juntos   ☮ #4

Pegamos al piso juntos,
Pegamos al piso juntos,
Pegamos al piso juntos,
Porque es divertido.

Aplaudimos juntos, (3×)
Porque es divertido.

Pateamos el piso juntos, (3×)
Porque es divertido.

Chocamos las rodillas, (3×)
Porque es divertido.

We wiggle our fingers together, (3×)
Because it's fun to do.

We all wave hello, (3×)
Because it's fun to do.

By Barbara Cass-Beggs

Movemos los dedos juntos, (3×)

Porque es divertido.

Saludamos hola, (3×)
Porque es divertido.

Translation by Rosa Hernandez and Gilda Martinez

11 "Eency Weency Spider"/ "Great Big Spider"   ⊛ #5

(With spider puppets)
The eency weency spider
Crawled up the water spout.
Down came the rain
And washed the spider out.
Out came the sun
And dried up all the rain.
And the eency weency spider
Went up the spout again.

(Sing in a deep voice with exaggerated movements)
The great big spider
Crawled up the water spout.
Down came the rain
And washed the spider out.
Out came the sun
And dried up all the rain.
And the great big spider
Went up the spout again.

Traditional; adapted by Barbara Cass-Beggs

12 "La araña pequeñita"/ "La araña grandotota"   ⊛ #5

(Con títeres de arañas)
La araña pequeñita
Subió subió subió.
Vino la lluvia
Y se la llevó.
Salió el sol
Y todo lo secó.
La araña pequeñita
Subió subió subió.

(Cante en una voz profunda con movimientos exagerados)
La araña grandotota
Subió subió subió.
Vino la lluvia
Y se la llevó.
Salió el sol
Y todo lo secó.
La araña grandotota
Subió subió subió.

Traditional

ADDITIONAL RHYMES

RIMAS ADICIONALES

13 "Two Little Dickey Birds"

Two little dickey birds sitting on a cloud,
One named "Soft," and one named "Loud."

14 "Dos pajaritos"

Dos pajaritos sentados en un nube,

Se llama "Bajito," se llama "Altito."

Fly away, Soft. Fly away, Loud.

Come back, Soft. Come back, Loud.

By Barbara Cass-Beggs

Véte, Bajito. Véte, Altito.

Vuelve, Bajito. Vuelve, Altito.

Translation by Anne Calderón

15 "Eeney Meeny Miney Moe"

Eeney meeny miney moe
Catch a tiger by the toe.
If he growls, let him go,
Eeney meeny, miney moe.
And out goes Y-O-U

And you are it, period,

Stamp, stamp it!

Traditional

16 "Pico pico solorico"

Pico pico solorico
¿Quién te dió tamaño pico?
La gallina, la jabada,
Puso un huevo en la quebrada.
Pusa uno, pusa dos, puso tres, puso cuatro,
Puso cinco, puso seis, puso siete, puso ocho;
Guarda tu bizcocho
Hasta mañana a las ocho.

Traditional from Venezuela

3. Body Rhymes   ⊚ #5

HEAD

17 "Where Is My Head?" ⊚ #5

Where is my head?
Knock, knock, here it is.
Where are my ears?
Tickle, tickle, here they are.
Where is my nose?
Here it is!

By Rosa Hernandez, Betsy Diamant-Cohen

FINGERS

19 "Fingers Like to Wiggle Waggle"   ⊚ #5

(Begin each verse by wiggling fingers of both hands in front of you)

3. Rimas del cuerpo ⊚ #5

CABEZA

18 "¿Dónde está mi cabeza?"
⊚ #5

¿Dónde está mi cabeza?
Ton, ton, aquí está.
¿Dónde están mis orejas?
Hacen cosquillas, cosquillas.
¿Dónde está mi naríz?
¡Aquí, tócala asi!

Translation by Rosa Hernandez, Gilda Martinez, and Gilda Valdes

LOS DEDITOS

20 "A los deditos les gusta moverse"   ⊚ #5

(Empiece cada verso moviendo sus dedos delante de usted)

Fingers like to wiggle waggle,
Wiggle waggle, wiggle waggle.
Fingers like to wiggle waggle
Way up high!
*(Continue wiggling fingers while
reaching straight up; say "high" in a
very high voice)*
Fingers like to wiggle waggle,
Wiggle waggle, wiggle waggle.
Fingers like to wiggle waggle
Way down low!
*(Continue wiggling fingers while
lowering hands; say "low" in a very
low voice)*
Fingers like to wiggle waggle,
Wiggle waggle, wiggle waggle.
Fingers like to wiggle waggle
On my knees!
(Place fingers on knees)

By Barbara Cass-Beggs

A los deditos les gusta moverse,
Asi asá, asi asá.
A los deditos les gusta moverse
¡Hacía arriba!
*(Siga moviendo sus deditos en lo que
estira sus brazos para arriba; Diga
"arriba" en voz alta)*
A los deditos les gusta moverse,
Asi asá, asi asá.
A los deditos les gusta moverse
¡Hacía abajo!
*(Continúe moviendo los deditos y baje
las manos; figa "abajo" en una voz
bien baja)*
A los deditos les gusta moverse,
Asi asá, asi asá.
A los deditos les gusta moverse
¡Sobre las rodillas!
(Ponga sus deditos en sus rodillas)

**Translation by Jennifer Bown-
Olmedo, Gilda Martinez, and Evelio
Méndez**

21 "Here Are Baby's Fingers"

Here are baby's fingers.
Here are baby's toes.
Here is baby's tummy button
Round and around it goes!

By Barbara Cass-Beggs

22 "Aqui están tus deditos"

Aqui están tus deditos.
Aqui estás tus pies.
Aqui está tu ombliguíto
Que te pore de revés.

Translation by Evelio Méndez

HANDS

23 "Here Are My Hands" ☻ #5

Here are my hands.
(Show open hands)
Where are my hands?
(Put hands behind back)

Let's take a peek.
(One hand over eyes, peering)
They're playing hide-and-seek!

MANITAS

24 "Tengo manitas"   ☻ #5

Tengo manitas
(Abra las manos)
No tengo manitas.
*(Esconda las manos atrás de su
espalda)*
Porque las tengo.
(Abra las manos)
Desconchabadita.

(Show open hands again)

Translation by Betsy Diamant-Cohen

25 "Little Tortillas for Mother/ Potatoes and Potatoes"   ☺ #5

(Slap hands together as if making tortillas)
Little tortillas for mama.
Little tortillas for papa.
The warm ones for mama.
The nice ones for papa.
Potatoes, potatoes for papa.
Potatoes, potatoes for mama.
The nice ones are for papa.
The warm ones are for mama.

Translation by Rosa Hernandez

27 "Open Them, Shut Them"

(Follow the instructions for your hands in the song)
Open them, shut them, (2×)
Give a little clap.
Open them, shut them, (2×)
Put them in your lap.
Creep them, creep them (2×)
Right up to your chin,
Open up your little mouth,
And do not let them in.

Traditional

29 "Show Ten Hands and Show Ten Fingers"
(Tune of "Ten Little Indians")

Show two hands and show ten fingers,
Show two hands and show ten fingers,

(Esconda las manos atrás de su espalda)

Traditional

26 "Tortillitas para mamá/ Papas y papas"   ☺ #5

(Pegue las manos como si estuviera haciendo tortillitas)
Tortillitas para mamá.
Tortillitas para papá.
Las doraditas para mamá.
Las bonitas para papá.
Papas y papas para papá.
Papas y papas para mamá.
Las bonitas para papá,
Las calientitas para mamá.

Traditional

28 "Abrelas, cierraleas"

(Siga las instrucciones de la canción para las manos)
Abrelas, cierralas, (2×)
Da un pequeño aplauso-so.
Abrelas, cierralas, (2×)
Ponlas en tu falda-da-da.
Pásalas, pásalas, (2×)
Hasta tu barbilla-la.
Abre tu boquita-ta,
No las dejes entrar.

Translation by Evelio Méndez

30 "Dos manitas, diez deditos"

(La melodia de "Diez indios")

Dos manitas, diez deditos,

Dos manitas, diez deditos,

Show two hands and show ten fingers,
Show them to your friends.
1 little, 2 little, 3 little fingers,
4 little, 5 little, 6 little fingers,
7 little, 8 little, 9 little fingers,
And one more makes ten!

Translation by Betsy Diamant-Cohen

Dos manitas, diez deditos,

Cuéntalos conmigo.
1, 2, 3 deditos,
4, 5, 6 deditos,
7, 8, 9 deditos,
¡Y uno más son diez!

Traditional

TICKLE RHYMES

31 "The Little Train Ran Up the Track"
(To be used with knee bounces)

The little train ran up the track.
(Walk fingers up baby's body from toes on one foot up to head)

It went toot, toot
(Gently tap baby's head twice)

And then it came back.
(Quickly tickle baby's body from head to toe)

Another train ran up the track.
(Walk fingers up baby's body starting with toes on other foot)

It went toot, toot
(Gently tap baby's head twice)

And then it came back.
(Quickly tickle baby's body from head to toe)

By Barbara Cass-Beggs

RIMAS DE COSQUILLAS

32 "El trencito ya corrió"

(Para usar con las canciones de movimiento de rodilla)

El trencito ya corrió.
(Camina los dedos suyos desde los dedos de un pie de su bebe hasta la cabeza de su bebe)
Hizo pa, pa
(Toca la cabeza de su bebe suavemente dos veces)
Y regresó.
(Rápidamente hágale cosquilla a su bebe desde la cabeza hasta los pies)
El otro trencito también ve corrió.
(Camina los dedos suyos desde los dedos de el otro pie de su bebe hasta la cabeza de su bebe)
Hizo pu, pu
(Toca la cabeza de su bebe suavemente dos veces)
Y regresó.
(Rápidamente hágale cosquilla a su bebe desde la cabeza hasta los pies)

Translation of lyrics by Evelio Méndez and directions by Gilda Martinez

KNEES

33 "This Is the Way the Ladies Ride"   ◉ #5

RODILLAS

34 "Así al caballo montan las damas"   ◉ #5

(Say each phrase faster than the one before)
This is the way the ladies ride . . .
Lim, lim, lim
This is way the gentlemen ride . . .
Trim, trim, trim
This is the way the farmers ride . . .
Trot, trot, trot
Sometimes they jump the fence
And sometimes they fall to the ground!

Translation to English by Anne Calderón and Rahel

(Diga cada frase un poquito mas rápido)
Así al caballo montan las damas,
Ta ta ta
Así cabalgan los caballeros,
Ta ta ta
Así montan los campesinos,
Ta ta ta
A veces saltan la barrera
A veces chocan con la tierra.

Traditional

35 "Giddy-Up My Horse" ☉ #5

Giddy-up my horse, hey! (3×)
Jump up high!

Giddy-up my horse, hey! (3×)
Don't fall down!

Giddy-up my horse, hey! (3×)
Here we go over!

By Rosa Hernandez and Rahel

36 Ándale caballo   ☉ #5

Ándale caballo, (3x)
¡Hacia arriba!

Ándale caballo, (3x),
¡Hacia abajo!

Ándale caballo, (3x),
¡Hacia al lado!

Translation by Rosa Hernandez, Gilda Martinez, and Gilda Valdes

37 "Jack and Jill"   ☉ #5

Jack and Jill went up the hill
(Bounce child on lap)
To fetch a pail of water.
Jack fell down,
(Lean to one side)
And rolled around
(Lean to the other side)
And Jill went tumbling after.
(Bounce very quickly!)

Traditional, adapted

38 "Juan y Juana"   ☉ #5

Juan y Juana subieron al monte
(Brinque el bebe en el regazo)
En busca de un cubo de agua.
Juan se cayó,
(Inclínese para un lado)
La crisma se rompió,
(Inclínese para el otro lado)
Y Juana se despeñó en la zanja.
(Brinque rápidamente)

Translation by Evelio Méndez

39 "Mother and Father and Uncle John"

Mother and Father and Uncle John

40 "Mamá, papá y el tío Juan"

Mamá, papá y el tío Juan,

Went to town, one by one.
(Bounce child on outstretched legs)

Mother fell off . . .
(Lean to one side)
And father fell off . . .
(Lean to the other side)
But Uncle John went on and on
and on and on and on and on . . .
(Bounce rapidly)

Traditional

Fueron al campo a jugar.
(Rebote el nino con sus piernes estiradas)
Mamá se cayó . . .
(Inclínese para un lado)
Papá se durmió . . .
(Inclínese para el otro lado)
Pero el tío Juan siguió y siguió . . .

(Brinque rápidamente)

Translation by Evelio Méndez

4. Rum Pum Pum Drum Sequence ☺ #6

41 "Rum Pum Pum" ☺ #6

(Children tap out names with syllables)
Rum pum pum.
This is my drum.
Rum pum pum.
This is my drum.
My name is ___. What's your name?

By Barbara Cass-Beggs

4. Sequencia de "rum pum peta" ☺ #6

42 "Rum pum peta" ☺ #6

(Los niños dan golpecitos para cada sílaba de su nombre)
Rum pum peta.
Escucha mi pandereta.
Rum pum peta.
Escucha mi pandereta.
Mi nombre es ___. ¿Y tu?

Translation by Anne Calderón

5. Standing-Up Activities ☺ #7

43 "And We Walk" ☺ #7

 And we walk, and we walk, and we walk, and we stop. (3×)
And we all turn around!
WHOOOO!

And we run, and we run, and we run, and we stop. (3×)
And we all turn around! WHOOOO!
(Shake the tambourine vigorously while everyone turns around)

5. Actividades al pararse ☺ #7

44 "Y caminamos" ☺ #7

Y caminamos, caminamos, caminamos, y paramos. (3×)
¡Y demos una vuelta!
¡JUUUUU!

Y corremos, y corremos, y corremos, y paramos. (3×)
¡Y demos una vuelta! ¡JUUUUU!
(Mueva el tamborín mucho en lo que todo el mundo da una vuelta)

And we jump, and we jump, and
we jump, and we stop. (3×)
And we all turn around! WHOOOO!
*(Substitute "walk" with other words
and motions: "run," "creep," "tiptoe,"
"jump," "march," etc.)*

By Betsy Diamant-Cohen

Y brincamos, y brincamos, y
brincamos, y paramos. (3×)
¡Y demos una vuelta! ¡JUUUUU!
*(Substituya "camina" con otras
palabras y movimientos: "corremos,"
"arrastramos," "vayamos de puntillas,"
"brinquemos," "marchemos," etc.)*

**Translation by Anne Calderón, Rosa
Hernandez, Evelio Méndez**

45 "The Chirimbolo Game"
  ◉ #7

The chirimbolo game
How fun it is!
One foot, the other foot
One hand, the other hand
One elbow, the other elbow.
The nose and the mouth.

**Translation to English by Anne
Calderón**

46 "El juego chirimbolo"
  ◉ #7

El juego chirimbolo
¡Qué bonito es!
Un pie, otro pie,
Una mano, otra mano
Un codo, otro codo.
La nariz y la boca.

Traditional

47 "Stir It, Stir the Chocolate"
  ◉ #7

Stir it, stir it, stir the chocolate.
You have a peanut nose.
One, two, three, CHO!
One, two, three, CO!
One, two, three, LA!
One, two, three, TE!
Chocolate, chocolate!
Stir it, stir it, stir the chocolate!
(Lower voice and body)
Stir it, stir it, stir it, stir it,
Stir it, stir it, stir the
CHOCOLATE!
(Jump up and shout)
Now we eat the chocolate and sit
down.

**Translation to English by Anne
Calderón**

48 "Bate, bate, chocolate"
  ◉ #7

Bate, bate, chocolate.
Tu nariz de cacahuate.
Uno, dos, tres, ¡CHO!
Uno, dos, tres, ¡CO!
Uno, dos, tres, ¡LA!
Uno, dos, tres, ¡TE!
¡Chocolate, chocolate!
¡Bate, bate, chocolate!
(Baje la voz y el cuerpo)
Bate, bate, bate, bate,
Bate, bate, ¡CHOCOLATE!

(Brinque y grite)
Y ahora comemos el chocolate y
nos sentamos.

Traditional

ADDITIONAL RHYMES	RIMA ADICIONALES
49 "We're Marching to the Drum"	**50 "Marchamos al tambor"**
We're marching to the drum. We're marching to the drum. Hi-ho the derri-o We're marching to the drum.	Marchamos al tambor. Marchamos al tambor. Rom, rom, rom, rom Marchammos al tambor.
We're marching 'round the room. We're marching 'round the room. Hi-ho the derri-o We're marching 'round the room.	Marchamos alrededor. Marchamos alrededor. Rom, rom, rom, rom Marchammos alrededor.
We're marching to the drum. We're marching to the drum. Hi-ho the derri-o We're marching to the drum.	Marchamos al tambor. Marchamos al tambor. Rom, rom, rom, rom Marchamos al tambor.
And the drum says "STOP."	Y el tambor dice "PARÓ."
Now we're going to run to the rhythm of the drum.	Ahora vamos a correr al ritmo del tambor.
We're running to the drum . . . We're creeping to the drum . . .	Corramos al tambor . . . Arrastramos al tambor . . .
Adapted by Barbara Cass-Beggs	**Translation by Evelio Méndez**
51 "Head, Shoulders, Knees, and Toes"	**52 Cabeza hombros, rodillas y pies**
Head, shoulders, knees and toes, knees and toes. (2×) And eyes and ears and mouth and nose. Head, shoulders, knees and toes, knees and toes.	Cabeza, hombros, rodillas y pies, rodillas y pies. (2×) Ojos, orejas, boca y nariz. Cabeza, hombros, rodillas y pies, rodillas y pies.
Traditional	**Traditional**
53 "Little Johnny Dances"	**54 "Juanito"**
Little Johnny dances, He dances, dances, dances. Little Johnny dances.	Juanito cuando baila, Baila, baila, baila. Juanito cuando baila.

He dances with his pinky.
With his pinky, pinky, pinky
That is how he dances.
(Substitute with: his "foot," "knee,"
"hip," "hand," "elbow," "shoulder,"
"head")

Translation by Betsy Diamant-Cohen

Baila con del dedito
Con el dedito, ito, ito
Asi baila Juanito.
(Substituye con: " el pie," "las rodilla,"
"la cadera," "la mano," "el codo," "el
hombro," "la cabeza")

Traditional

55 "Handy Spandy"
(To be used with Standing-Up
Activities)

Handy Spandy, sugar and candy,
we all jump in.
Handy Spandy, sugar and candy,
we all jump out.
Handy Spandy, sugar and candy,
we all jump up.
Handy Spandy, sugar and candy,
we all sit down.

Traditional

56 "Maria Antonia"
(Para usar con las canciones de
pararse)

Maria Antonia, azucar y dulce,
brinquemos adentro.
Maria Antonia, azucar y dulce,
todos brinquemos fulera.
Maria Antonia, azucar y dulce,
brinquemos hacia arriba.
Maria Antonia, azucar y dulce,
ahora nos sentamos.

Translation by Jennifer Bown-Olmedo and Evelio Méndez

6. Animals! 💿 #8

6. ¡Animales! 💿 #8

57 "I Went to Visit the Farm"
💿 #8

I went to visit a farm one day.
I saw a horse along the way.
And what do you think the horse
did say?
["Neigh, neigh."]
(Substitute: "cat," "cow," "sheep," "pig,"
"dog," "duck," "rooster")

Anonymous

58 "Fui a visitar la granja"
💿 #8

Fui a visitar la granja un día.
Por allí vi un caballo.
¿Qué crees que dijo el caballo?

["Jeeee, jeeee."]
(Substituye: "gato," "vaca," "oveja,"
"cerdo," "perro," "pato," "gallo")

Translation by Anne Calderón

59 "When the [Cats] Get Up in the Morning" 💿 #8

When the [cats] get up in the
morning, they always say "[Meow]!"

60 "Cuando los [gatos] se despiertan" 💿 #8

Cuando los [gatos] se despiertan,
siempre dicen "[¡Miau!]"

When the [cats] get up in the morning, they say, "[Meow, meow]!"
(Substitute: "dogs," "cows," "horses," "pigs," "roosters," "hens," "ducks," "geese")

By Barbara Cass-Beggs

Cuando los [gatos] se despiertan, siempre dicen "[¡Miau, miau!]"

(Substituye: "perros," "vacas," "caballos," "cerdos," "gallos," "gallinas," "patos," "gansos")

Translation by Anne Calderón and Gilda Martinez

61 "One Elephant Went Out to Play" ☻ #8

One elephant went out to play
Upon a spider's web one day.
He had such enormous fun
That he called for another elephant to come.

Two elephants went out to play
Upon a spider's web one day.
They had such enormous fun
That they called for another elephant to come.

Traditional

62 "Un elefante se balanceaba" ☻ #8

Un elefante se balanceaba
Sobre la tela de una araña.
Como veía que resistía
Fue a llamar a otro elefante.

Dos elefantes se balanceaban
Sobre la tela de una araña.
Como veían que resistía
Fueron a llamar a otro elefante.

Traditional

63 "Hickory Dickory Dare" ☻ #8

Hey, look over there!
The pig flew up in the air!
(Throw a stuffed animal pig into the air)
Farmer Brown soon brought her down,
 Hickory, dickory dare.

Traditional; adapted by Betsy Diamant-Cohen

64 "El cochinito" ☻ #8

¡Mire el cochinito!
¡Voló por el aire!
(Tire el cerdo de peluche al aire)

Muy pronto lo bajó

¡Ay! hacer un baile.

Translation by Rosa Hernandez, Iris Cotto, Gilda Martinez, and Gilda Valdes

7. Musical Instruments and Props ☻ #9, #10

BELLS

7. Instrumentos musicales y accesorios ☻ #9, #10

BELLS

65 "We Ring Our Bells Together" ☉ #9

We ring our bells together,
We ring our bells together,
We ring our bells together,
Because it's fun to do. (2×)
Ring them up HIGH.
Ring them down LOW.
Ring them in the MIDDLE.

By Barbara Cass-Beggs

66 "Toquemos campanillas" ☉ #9

Toquemos campanillas,
Toquemos campanillas.
Toquemos campanillas,
Porque es divertido. (2×)
Tócalas ARRIBA.
Tócalas ABAJO.
Tócalas en el MEDIO.

Translation by Anne Calderón

67 "Are You Sleeping, Brother John? (Frère Jacques)" ☉ #9

Are you sleeping? Are you sleeping?
Brother John, Brother John?
Morning bells are ringing (2×)
Ding dang dong (2×)

Traditional

68 "Martinillo (Frère Jacques)" ☉ #9

Martinillo, Martinillo
¿Dónde estás? ¿Dónde estás?
Toca la campana (2×)
Din don dan (2×)

Traditional

69 "Teresa, the Queen" ☉ #9

Teresa, the queen,
Tippiti tippiti teen.
Upon her head a crown,
(Put your hands above your head in the shape of a crown)
Tippiti tippiti town.

She rings four bells,
Tippiti tippiti tells.
She tiptoes here and there,
Tippiti tippiti tear.

Translation to English by Gilda Martinez and Betsy Diamant-Cohen

70 "Teresa, la marquesa" ☉ #9

Teresa, la marquesa,
Tipiti, tipitesa.
Tenia una corona,
(Ponga sus manos arriba de su cabeza como si fuera una corona)
Tipiti, tipitona.

Con cuatro campanillas,
Tipiti, tipitillas.
Y caminaba de puntillas,
Tipiti tipiton.

Traditional

71 "Bells Away" ☉ #9

Bells away, bells away

72 "Entréguenlas campanas" ☉ #9

Entréguenlas, entréguenlas

Put the bells away today.

By Barbara Cass-Beggs

Pongamos todo en su lugar.

Translation by Anne Calderón

ADDITIONAL RHYMES

73 "Bells Go in the Bag"
(To the tune of "We Hit the Floor Together")

Bells go in the bag, (3×)
Because it's fun to do.

Adapted by Betsy Diamant-Cohen

75 "We Shake Our Maracas Together"

We shake our maracas together,
We shake our maracas together,
We shake our maracas together,
Because it's fun to do.
Shake them up high.
Shake them down low.
Shake them in the middle.

By Barbara Cass-Beggs

77 "Underneath a Button"

Underneath a button
In Mr. Martin's house, house,
He found a tiny, tiny,
Hidden little mouse, mouse.
What a little tiny,
Tiny, tiny, mouse, mouse,
Underneath a button,
In Mr. Martin's house, house.

Translation by Rosa Hernandez and
Betsy Diamant-Cohen

79 "Maracas in the Bag"
(To the tune of "We Hit the Floor Together")

RIMAS ADICIONALES

74 "Campanas a la bolsa"
(Con la melodía de "Peguemos el piso juntos")

Campanas a la bolsa, (3×)
Porque es divertido.

Translation by Evelio Méndez

76 "Sacudimos las maracas"

Sacudimos las maracas,
Sacudimos las maracas,
Sacudimos las maracas,
Porque es divertido.
Sacudimos arriba.
Sacudimos abajo.
Sacudimos en el medio.

Translation by Rosa Hernandez

78 "Debajo de un botón, ton"

Debajo de un botón, ton
Que encontró Martin, tin,
Habia un ratón, ton,
¡Ay! que chiquitín, tin.
Que tan chiquitín, tin,
Era aquél ratón, ton,
Que encontró Martin, tin,
Debajo de un botón, ton.

Traditional

80 "Maracas a la bolsa"
(Con la melodía de "Peguemos el piso juntos")

Maracas in the bag, (3×)
Because it's fun to do.

Adapted by Betsy Diamant-Cohen

81 "We Tap Our Sticks Together"

We tap our sticks together
Tap our sticks together,
Tap our sticks together,
Because it's fun to do.

By Barbara Cass-Beggs

83 "Grandfather's Clock"

Grandfather's clock goes . . .
Tic-toc, tic-toc, tic-toc.
(Tap sticks very slowly)
 Mother's kitchen clock goes . . .
 Tic-toc, tic-toc, tic-toc, tic-toc.
(Tap at moderate tempo)
Baby's little clock goes . . .
Tic-toc, tic-toc, tic-toc, tic-toc, tic-toc.
STOP!

(Tap rapidly)

By Barbara Cass Beggs

85 "Sticks Away"

Sticks away, sticks away
Put your sticks away today.

By Barbara Cass Beggs

SCARVES

87 "Wind, Oh Wind"   ☻ #10

Wind, oh wind, oh wind, I say,
What are you blowing away today?
Scarves, oh scarves, oh scarves, I say.

Maracas a la bolsa, (3×)
Porque es divertido.

Translation by Evelio Méndez

82 "Suena los palitos"

Suena los palitos,
Suena los palitos,
Suena los palitos,
Porque es divertido.

Translation by Anne Calderón, Evelio Méndez, and Gilda Martinez

84 "El reloj"

El reloj de abuelo suena . . .
Tic-toc, tic-toc, tic-toc.
(Suene los palos léntamente)
El reloj de mamá suena . . .
Tic-toc tic-toc, tic-toc tic-toc.
(Suene los palos)
El relojito del niñito suena . . .
Tic-toc tic-toc tic-toc tic-toc, tic-toc.
¡PARE!

(Suene los palos rápidamente)

Translation by Anne Calderón

86 "Palitos a la bolsa"

Palitos, palitos
Palitos a la bolsa.

Translation by Evelio Méndez

PAÑUELOS

88 "Viento, ay viento"   ☻ #10

Viento, viento, viento siento,
¿Qué vas a llevar hoy?
Pañuelo, pañuelo, pañuelo, al suelo.

The wind is blowing the scarves away.

By Barbara Cass-Beggs

El viento lleva el pañuelo al suelo.

Translation by Anne Calderón

89 "Peek-a-Boo, I See You" ⊙ #10

Peek-a-boo, I see you! I see you smiling there. (2×)
(Walk around circle playing scarf peek-a-boo with each child)

By Barbara Cass-Beggs

90 "Peek-a-boo" ⊙ #10

Peek-a-boo, ¿Quién está, quién está allí? (2×)
(Ande alrededor y jueuge peek a boo con cada niño)

Translation by Anne Calderón and Rosa Hernandez

91 "This Is the Way We Wash" ⊙ #10

This is the way we wash our face, wash our face, wash our face, This is the way we wash our face, so early in the morning.
(Substitute with: "neck," "arms," "knees")

Traditional

92 "Así vamos a lavarnos" ⊙ #10

Así vamos a lavarnos la cara, lavarnos la cara, lavarnos la cara, Así vamos a lavarnos la cara, con el pañuela.
(Substituye con: "cuella," "brazos," "rodillas")

Translation by Anne Calderón

93 "Scarves Away" ⊙ #10

Scarves away, scarves away
Put the scarves away today.

By Barbara Cass-Beggs

94 "Entréguenlos, entréguenlos" ⊙ #10

Entréguenlos, entréguenlos
Pongamos todo en su lugar.

Translation by Anne Calderón

8. Lullabies ⊙ #11

8. Cancioncitas ⊙ #11

95 "Twinkle, Twinkle, Little Star" ⊙ #11

(Sing slowly)
Twinkle, twinkle, little star
How I wonder where you are.
Up above the world so high
Like a diamond in the sky.

96 "Estrellita dónde estás" ⊙ #11

(Cante despacio)
Estrellita dónde estás
Me pregunto que serás.
En el cielo, en el mar
Un diamante de verdad.

Twinkle, twinkle, little star
How I wonder where you are.

Traditional

Estrellita, dónde estás
Me pregunto qué serás.

Traditional

9. Interactive Rhymes
◉ #12

9. Rimas interactivas
◉ #12

97 "Jack Be Nimble"   ◉ #12

Jack, be nimble!
Jack, be quick!
Jack, jump over
The candlestick.

Traditional

98 "¡Juan alerta!"   ◉ #12

¡Juan, alerta!
¡Juan, ligero!
Salta la vela
Y el candelero.

Translation by Anne Calderón

99 "Humpty Dumpty" ◉ #12

Humpty Dumpty sat on a wall.
Humpty Dumpty had a great fall.
(Sweep Humpy off of the wall with a large hand movement)
All the king's horses and all the king's men
Couldn't put Humpty together again.

Traditional

100 "Jamti Damti"   ◉ #12

Jamti Damti se sentó en un muro.
Jamti Damti se cayó muy duro.
(Quite a Jamti Damti de la pared con un movimiento grande)
Ni la guardia civil ni la caballería

Sabían cómo se incorporaría.

Translation by Anne Calderón

10. Closing Section ◉ #13

10. Despedida   ◉ #13

101 "Can You Kick with Two Feet?"   ◉ #13

Can you kick with two feet,
two feet, two feet?
Can you kick with two feet,
kick kick kick kick kick.

Can you kiss with two lips,
two lips, two lips?
Can you kiss with two lips,
mua mua mua mua mua.

102 "¿Puedes patear con dos pies?"   ◉ #13

¿Puedes patear con dos pies,
dos pies, dos pies?
Puedes patear con dos pies,
pa pa pa pa pa.

¿Puedes besar con dos labios,
dos labios, dos labios?
Puedes besar con dos labios,
mua mua mua mua mua.

Can you wave bye-bye, bye-bye, bye-bye? Can you wave bye-bye, bye-bye bye-bye bye.	¿Puedes decir adiós, adiós, adiós? Puedes decir adiós, adiós, adiós.
Traditional	**Translation by Anne Calderón**

Program Resources

There are many wonderful resources for traditional Spanish nursery rhymes from around the world, including books, CD-ROMs, and Web sites. Many public libraries also publish their own flyers or booklets with Spanish rhymes that work well in early childhood programs. Some of my favorite resources are listed.

Books

Arrorró, mi niño, by Lulu Delacre. New York: Lee & Low Books, 2009.

De colores and Other Latin American Folksongs for Children (Anthology), by José-Luis Orozco. New York: Puffin, 1999.

Diez deditos and Other Play Rhymes and Action Songs from Latin America, by Elisa Kleven and José-Luis Orozco. New York City: Puffin, 2002.

Los pollitos dicen/The Baby Chicks Sing, by Nancy Abraham Hall and Jill Syverson-Stork. New York: Little, Brown, 1994.

Mamá Gansa, by Michael Hague. Corunna, Spain: Everest de Ediciones y Distribución, 1998.

¡Pío peep: Traditional Spanish Nursery Rhymes, by Alma Flor Ada, F. Isabel Campoy, and Alice Schertle. ABRIL: Rayo, 2003.

Read Me a Rhyme in Spanish and English/Léame una rima en Español e Ingles, by Rose Zertuche Treviño. Atlanta: ALA Editions, 2009.

Riqui, riqui, riqui, ran: Canciones para jugar y bailar (Cilleccion clave de sol) (Spanish Edition), by David Márquez. Caracas: Ediciones Ekare, 2003.

Tortillitas para mamá and Other Nursery Rhymes (Bilingual Edition in Spanish and English), by Margot C. Griego, Betsy L. Bucks, Sharon S. Gilbert, and Laurel H. Kimball. New York: Henry Holt, 1988.

CDs

Cantoalegre De Paseo, by multiple artists. Medellin: Discos Fuentes, 1983. Available: www.discosfuentes.com/index.php?main_page=product_info&products_id=25503.

Children's Nursery Rhyme Songs in Spanish: Canciones infantiles para niños en Español. Bilingual Beginnings, 2004. Available: www.BilingualBeginnings.net.

De Colores and Other Latin American Folk Songs for Children, by José-Luis Orozco. Arcoiris Records, 1996.

Escucha y Disfruta con Mama Gansa / Listen, Like, Learn with Mother Goose on the Loose, by Betsy Diamant-Cohen. Betsy's Folly Studios, 2009. Available: www.cdbaby.com/cd/rembdc.

Lírica Infantil, Vol. 4: *Animales & Movimiento*, by José-Luis Orozco. Arcoiris Records, 2000.

Lírica Infantil, Vol. 8: *Arrullos: Lullabies in Spanish*, by José-Luis Orozco. Arcoiris Records, 2000.

Trepsi, Vol. 3. Centro de estimulación y desarrollo infantil, 2001. Available: www.trepsi.com.mx.

Trepsi, Vol. 4. Centro de estimulación y desarrollo infantil, 2003. Available: www.trepsi.com.mx.

Trepsi, Vol. 6: *Los Colores*. Centro de estimulación y desarrollo infantil, 2007. Available: www.trepsi.com.mx.

Trepsi, Vol. 7: *Los Transportes*. Centro de estimulación y desarrollo infantil, 2002. Available: www.trepsi.com.mx.

Web Sites

Bilingual Journey—Everything in Spanish for the Bilingual Child. Available: www.bilingualjourney.com (accessed August 2, 2009). This is a great resource for purchasing children's materials in Spanish, and it has links to many other useful sites.

Mamá Lisa's World of Children and International Culture. Available: www.mamalisa.com (accessed August 2, 2009). This is Lisa Yannucci's Web site.

Songs for Teaching: Using Music to Promote Learning. "EFL/ESOL/ESL Songs and Activities: Song Lyrics for Teaching English as a Second Language." Available: http://songsforteaching.com/esleflesol.htm (accessed August 2, 2009).

Worthington Libraries. "Programs to Go: Kids." Available: www2.worthingtonlibraries.org/programs2go/browse.cfm?section_id=1 (accessed August 3, 2009). The list of songs and rhymes in English and Spanish includes helpful audio and video clips.

Barbara Cass-Beggs Rhymes in English

Folk Lullabies, by Barbara Cass-Beggs and Michael Beggs. New York: Oak Publications, 1969.

Your Baby Needs Music, by Barbara Cass-Beggs. New York: Addison Wesley, 1990.

Your Child Needs Music: A Complete Course in Teaching Music to Children, by Barbara Cass-Beggs. Mississauga, Ontario, Canada: Frederick Harris Music Co., 1986.

Chapter 14

Developmental Tips in English and Spanish

Developmental tips play an extremely important role in Mother Goose on the Loose en Español. The audience in any beginning parenting program with both English and non-English speakers may be unfamiliar with parenting techniques; positive reinforcement; the importance of reading to, singing to, and playing with their children; and basic child development. They may not know when to discipline and when not to. Parenting books may not be the answer, because some program attendees may be illiterate. Non-English speakers may be embarrassed to speak with native English speakers and, as a result, may isolate themselves rather than making use of all the free resources available to them. The best way to combat this is by consistently being friendly and welcoming to everyone and to include developmental tips in the language of program attendees during your Mother Goose on the Loose en Español programs.

Often parents want to do the best they can for their children, but they are not quite sure what is involved. The developmental tip, a very short phrase that focuses on some aspect of child development, parenting, or school readiness, helps improve understanding of the things their child is doing, the activities that can help their child develop early literacy skills, the importance of such activities and skills, and ways to replicate them at home.

For instance, parents may want their child to be well-behaved, but they might not realize that a two year old cannot sit still. Their response, then, will be to punish the two year old for exploring a room rather than sitting in one place without fidgeting. To address this, there is a developmental tip built into the welcoming comments each week designed to put parents at ease by alerting them to the fact that two year olds do not sit still.

This tip, however, is part of the prepackaged program, because it is scripted into the welcoming comments. Other developmental tips are not built into the weekly script. Instead, each presenter is urged to choose two developmental tips per session to add into their program. These tips can be connected with some part of the program and offered to adults in an informal manner. For instance, a tip that encourages positive physical bonding between adult and child might focus on the fact that when children are rocked and held close enough to their adult so they can hear a steady heartbeat, it reminds them of the time when they were in the womb and helps them to calm down. A tip about the value of knee bounces, making the correlation between the steady beat of the bounce and the beating of the heart when the child was still in utero, might encourage an adult who generally sets the child beside him to actually put the child on his lap and try bouncing together.

Another type of developmental tip is informational, explaining aspects of school readiness. For instance, when giving instructions for pulling Humpy Dumpty off of his wall, the presenter might add a tip about the importance of self-regulation for school readiness. The presenter might describe the way children are invited to come up to the flannel board at their own pace, to take just one turn pulling Humpty off of his wall, and to applaud for all children when they do the same thing. The developmental tip can connect these actions with the way children are expected to act in a school classroom—taking turns, showing respect to each other, learning to stand in front of the class and fulfill the teacher's request. This tip shows parents how simple activities can be used to build a child's social and emotional skills.

During the Rum Pum Pum Drum Sequence, the developmental tip might use the words "phonological awareness" and explain to parents that children who can hear sounds in words have an easier time learning how to read. Parents can then be urged to create activities at home where children can tap out the names of things on pots and pans.

A developmental tip may explain that children find it very easy to imitate animal sounds and, by offering them the opportunity to do so, the parent is building up their interest in the world around them as well as providing opportunities for positive reinforcement. A tip that goes along with the song "I Went to Visit the Farm" while showing animal pictures from *The Very Busy Spider* may encourage parents to sing songs that correlate with a book's illustrations without actually reading the book. This type of developmental tip explains that books do not always need to be read aloud for them to be of value; simply looking at the pictures and singing a song about them is worthwhile. The tip might then include examples of why this is valuable: it gives children a joyful experience with books, it encourages them to "read" the picture in order to determine which sound to make (and recognizing their knowledge of the appropriate sounds for each animal builds their self-confidence), and it gives them the opportunity to feel comfortable in displaying their knowledge to others. Adults might then be reminded that the library has many books with animal illustrations and encouraged to borrow some of these books in order to repeat the activity at home.

To recap, developmental tips have many useful functions, including the following:

- They help presenters facilitate interaction between adults and their children.
- They teach bits of child development (e.g., the fact that children age two and under cannot be expected to sit perfectly still).

- They explain what school readiness is.
- They explain why certain activities can be helpful in a child's early development.
- They offer practical suggestions for implementing activities outside of the library setting.
- They can give simple instructions for an upcoming activity.

The optimal number of developmental tips is two per session. Too many developmental tips can become overwhelming and didactic. Fewer than two is not enough! Below is a selection of developmental tips in both English and Spanish. The tips are presented in English first and then followed by their Spanish translation.

Write out the tips that you want to use on an index card. Put the cards in your pile of flannel board characters and books with illustrations to reflect the order in which you want to use them.

Sample Developmental Tips in English and Spanish

- Look at your child in the eyes when you sing. Don't forget to smile!
- Sit your child on your lap so he or she can feel the rhythm and movement.
- Use different emotions and tones of voice when reading to your child.
- Invent new words to your favorite song.
- Act out the storyline of a book or song with your child.
- Play "Simon Says" with your child.
- Sing to your child while you bathe him or her.
- Show your child the different parts of a book (cover, title, author, pages, etc.).
- Give your baby a musical instrument so he or she can participate also.
- By tapping their names on the drum, children become aware of syllables and sounds (called "phonological awareness"), which is an important pre-reading skill.

- Mire a su hijo en los ojos cuando canta. ¡No se olvide de sonreír!
- Siéntese con su hijo en la falda para que comparten un momento cariñoso.
- Cuando lee a su hijo, use entonaciones diferentes y exprésese con emoción.
- Invente palabras nuevas para sus canciones favoritas.
- Actúe con su hijo las acciones de que cuenta una canción o un libro.
- Juegue "Simón dice . . ." con su hijo.
- Cante a su hijo cuando le cambia el pañal y le baña.
- Muestrele a su hijo las partes de un libro antes de leer (la portada, el título, el autor, las páginas, etc.).
- Déles a los bebés instrumentos musicales para que participen también.
- Al darle palmaditas al tambor, los niños reconocerán el concepto de la sílaba y los sonidos (eso se llama "reconocimiento fonológico"), que es una destreza muy importante en la preparación para leer.

- "Stop" is a word that all young children need to learn. Rather than waiting to teach "stop" in situations that are urgent or when you are angry, try playing games that teach "stop" in a loving manner. Then, when you need your child to respond instantly to the "stop" command, it will already be preprogrammed in the brain without any type of negative connotations.

- A great way to promote reading is to read books aloud to your child.

- By naming parts of the body in songs, you can help your child become more familiar and comfortable with their own physical being.

- Games like "Humpty Dumpty" are great for teaching children the social skills of being patient and taking turns, which is really important for getting along with others and doing well in school.

- Singing a clean-up song makes cleaning up a fun activity for children and teaches them what behavior you expect when it is time to put something away. Cleaning up with a song is gentle and loving and makes the activity seems much more like fun than a chore.

- Songs with action help your child learn how to sing and move at the same time, developing musical skills though participation and total involvement. They also encourage accurate listening and singing.

- By repeating "Mother and Father and Uncle John" each week, children learn to connect the words with the learning motions. Even the youngest child learns how to anticipate when to lean.

- "Para" es una palabra que todos los niños tienen que aprender. En vez de tratar de enseñarles en concepto de "para" en situaciones urgentes o cuando está molesto, intente a hacer juegos que enseñan la palabra "para" de una manera cariñosa. Así que su hijo podrá responder inmediatamente al mandato sin ningún tipo de connotación negativa.

- Una buena manera de promover la lectura es leer libros en voz alta con su hijo.

- Cuando cante canciones que incluyen los nombres de las partes del cuerpo y ayudará a su hijo a conocer y sentir a gusto con su propio cuerpo.

- Los juegos como "Jamti Damti" son buenos para enseñarles a los niños las destrezas sociales de ser paciente y tomar turnos, los cuales son muy importantes para poder llevarse bien con los demás y salir adelante en la escuela.

- Cantando una canción de la limpieza hace que el limpiar sea una actividad divertida para los niños y los enseña cooperar cuando necesitan arreglar sus cosas. Arreglando los jugetes através de una canción es dócil y cariñoso y se parece más a un juego que un trabajo de la casa.

- Las canciones con acción ayudan a que su hijo aprenda a cantar y mover a la misma vez, desarrollando destrezas musicales a través de participación y participación total.

- La repetición semanal de las canciones ayudará a su hijo a hacer conexiones entre palabras y movimientos. Incluso el niño más pequeño aprende a anticipar los movimientos.

- Snuggle closely with your children as you sing a lullaby, so they can hear your heartbeat as you sing and rock with them. This will remind them of the time when they were still in your womb, and will help to calm them down.
- In addition to being loads of fun, knee-bouncing rhymes help children become aware of the underlying beat of music.

- Abrace a su hijo cuando canta la cancioncita para que pueda sentir el latido de su corazón. Le recordará de cuando todavía estaba en su vientre y le ayudará a tranquilizarse.

- Además de ser muy divertido, las rimas de movimiento en las piernas ayudan a los niños a ser concientes del ritmo de la música.

Additional Resources in Spanish

Colorin' Colorado: www.colorincolorado.org/guides/readingtips. This Web site provides one-page Reading Tip Sheets in English and Spanish.

Kid's Health: http://kidshealth.org/parent/en_espanol/esp_land_pg/spanish_landing_page .html. Kids Health from Nemours has information in Spanish and English that can be used for tips about social and emotional wellness as well as fitness and safety.

Reading Is Fundamental: www.rif.org/assets/Documents/parents/RIF_ParentBrochure_ Spanish_061807.pdf; www.rif.org/parents/tips/default.mspx. Reading Is Fundamental has downloadable brochures in Spanish that provide a wealth of developmental tips (first URL). They also have numerous tips that can be used if translated into Spanish by your community partner (second URL).

Washington Learning Center: www.walearning.com/Parent-Infant.html. Washington Learning Center has free learning sheets in English and Spanish that include some great developmental tips.

Additional Resources in English

Better Brains for Babies: www.fcs.uga.edu/ext/bbb/factSheets.php. This wonderful site is hosted by the University of Georgia.

The Center for Development and Learning: www.cdl.org/for_families/index.htm. This Web site's special section for families is rich in developmental tips.

The Early Literacy Kit: A Handbook and Developmental Tip Cards (Diamant-Cohen and Ghoting, ALA Editions, 2009). This book has more than 100 developmental tip cards that can easily be used in your Mother Goose on the Loose en Español program. Each card has one developmental tip combined with an associated rhyme or activity along with instructions for the librarian. These were specifically created for use in library programs such as Mother Goose on the Loose en Español.

The National Association for the Education of Young Children (NAEYC): www.naeyc .org/ece/eyly. This site features short articles on topics such as "Helping Toddlers Become Problem Solvers." Choose a few sentences to create a developmental tip, and ask your community partner to translate and present the tip.

Zero to Three: www.zerotothree.org/site/PageServer?pagename=par_parents. This extensive Web site includes tips for parents on multiple topics. Look at these tips and choose just a few sentences to use as a developmental tip in your program.

PART V

A Personal Word

Chapter 15

Final Thoughts

Creating and running these programs has been an exhilarating experience for me. Being part of the original Buena Casa, Buena Brasa program with Anne Calderón at the Enoch Pratt Free Library in Baltimore inspired me to develop a Spanish-language version of Mother Goose on the Loose. It is my hope that this book will inspire other librarians to begin presenting Mother Goose on the Loose en Español even if they do not speak Spanish themselves. This book is meant to simplify the process of planning and presenting these programs. I hope that those librarians who have not yet felt comfortable with running programs for English-language learners will be inspired to dive right in!

Although this book stands alone as a guide to help create and run successful Spanish-language programs in your library (even if you don't speak Spanish), it can easily be used in conjunction with the original Mother Goose on the Loose manual published by Neal-Schuman (2006). That binder includes a plethora of songs by Barbara Cass-Beggs, more developmental tips, clear explanations regarding school readiness and early literacy skills, and ten complete scripts for English-language Mother Goose on the Loose programs. Everything you ever wanted know (except how to run Spanish-language programs when you don't speak Spanish) is covered there. The first edition remains a great resource and can provide much useful supplemental information to this book.

I am currently developing an interactive Web site for social networking via Mother Goose on the Loose in all of its aspects. Feel free to visit the site at www.mgol.org and check out the ever-growing tools available there. Through it, I hope to create a community of educators who will share materials as well as their passion and experience for all Mother Goose on the Loose programs. Also, a CD with over 100 songs (a combination of both English and Spanish) for use in Mother Goose on the Loose en Español is now available at http://cdbaby.com/cd/rembdc.

Last month, I met Anne at one of the Pratt libraries, and we ran a streamlined Mother Goose on the Loose en Español program together. Some of the moms from the original Buena Casa, Buena Brasa program were there. Because I no longer come on a regular basis, I had not seen them in quite awhile, and they greeted me with big hugs. Each mom told me that the children who had come to our very first programs were now in public school and doing very well. They proudly connected their family's attendance at our program to their children's success in elementary school. This was wonderful to hear! By offering Mother Goose on the Loose en Español at your library, I am sure that you will also hear similar uplifting stories, feel proud of the services you are offering, and form long-lasting bonds with your public.

¡Hasta luego!
Betsy

If you are interested in booking a training workshop for Mother Goose on the Loose or Mother Goose on the Loose en Español, please contact me at betsydc@mgol.org.

Title Index

Page numbers followed by the letter "f" indicate figures; those followed by the letter "t" indicate tables.

Subject Index

Page numbers followed by the letter "f" indicate figures.

About the Author

A graduate of Brandeis University, **Dr. Betsy Diamant-Cohen** earned her MLS from the Graduate School of Library and Information Science at Rutgers University and her Doctorate in Communications Design (DCD) from the University of Baltimore.

In the early 1980s, Diamant-Cohen worked as a children's librarian at public libraries in New Jersey. From 1986 to 1988, Diamant-Cohen served as a librarian in the Ruth Youth Wing of the Israel Museum in Jerusalem. She also was a part-time nursery school teacher and a storytime provider for the Municipality of Jerusalem and JELLY (Jerusalem English Language Libraries for Youth). She served as the Children's Programming Specialist for the Enoch Pratt Free Library for many years.

Dr. Diamant-Cohen received a citation by Maryland's Governor Glendenning for encouraging children to read in 1999. In 2002, the Enoch Pratt Free Library received the Godfrey Award for Excellence in Public Library Services for Families and Children, citing the importance of the Mother Goose on the Loose programs and training sessions offered. In 2004, *Library Journal* named Diamant-Cohen a "Mover and Shaker" in the library world. Her article "Mother Goose on the Loose: Applying Brain Research to Early Childhood Programs in the Public Library" won first prize for best feature article in *Public Libraries* magazine for 2004.

Diamant-Cohen is Executive Director of Mother Goose on the Loose, LLC and hopes to help Mother Goose on the Loose become available to librarians around the world. For more information about Diamant-Cohen and Mother Goose on the Loose, visit her Web site (www.mgol.org).

Diamant-Cohen lives in Baltimore, Maryland, with her husband Stuart, three children, two cats, and many stuffed animal frogs.